TOTAL SURRENDER

Total Surrender

Mother Teresa
Edited by
Brother Angelo Devananda Scolozzi

SERVANT
BOOKS

PUBLISHED BY ST. ANTHONY MESSENGER PRESS
CINCINNATI, OHIO

In the original edition of the work, the title was *Mother Teresa:
Contemplative in the Heart of the World*. In this revised edition,
the title is *Total Surrender*.

Cover design by Michael Andaloro
Cover photo by Raghu Rai/MAGNUM

ISBN-13: 978-0-89283-651-2
ISBN-10: 0-89283-651-2

Published by Servant Books, an imprint of
St. Anthony Messenger Press
28 W. Liberty St.
Cincinnati, OH 45202
www.ServantBooks.org

Printed in the United States of America

09   22 21 20

Dedication

To Mary, the Mother of Jesus and our Mother

Something Beautiful for God

Come with me into a world of poverty,
Into a land where men are dying endlessly,
Into a world of inhumanity.
Can't you see they're starving, where's your
    charity.
They laugh and cry, they're people just like
    you and me,
They need help and not just sympathy.

Chorus:
Show each one something beautiful for
    God above,
Something beautiful to show your love,
Something beautiful for God above,
Something beautiful to show your love.

A day goes by, the night is long for everyone,
A child is crying, perhaps he'll live to see
    the sun,
And yet he knows the morning may
    not come.

Throughout the world our brothers live
   in poverty,
They're everywhere if only we have eyes
   to see,
So look around and find your sanity.

Show to men the love that he has shown
   to you,
And feed his lambs as he has fed each one
   of you,
He loves them as much as he loves you.

Contents

ACKNOWLEDGMENTS

I WOULD LIKE TO THANK TWO PEOPLE who really are at the root of this book. Bert Ghezzi, the former editorial director of Servant Publications who first proposed the idea for this book, and Ann Spangler, the current editorial director of Servant Publications, who helped me bring the idea to birth through her editing skill, perseverance, and hard work. I consider each a real brother and sister in the Lord.

Note to the Reader

TOTAL SURRENDER IS THE REVISED edition of *Mother Teresa: Contemplative in the Heart of the World.*

The selections have been extracted from the following sources: The Constitution of the Missionary of Charity Sisters; The Explanation of the Original Constitution, edited by Sister Nirmala and based on the words of Mother Teresa; Mother's Instructions to the Sisters; Mother Teresa's Instructions to Superiors, Tertians, and Novices; and Mother's General Letters to the Sisters. Selections from the constitution appear in italics. The song "Something Beautiful for God," reprinted after the dedication, was written by one of the Missionaries of Charity and is taken from the Missionary of Charity Songbook.

These extracts remain the right and property of Mother Teresa.

It should be noted that the essential aspects of Mother Teresa's spiritual vision and way of life have been settled from the time she left the convent of the Loreto nuns to live on the second floor of Michael and Agnes Gomez's home in Creek Lane. And it is also true that the constitution contains the essence of her teaching. Everything else flows from it and points back to it. As Mother has said: "The simplicity and humility that prevails in the Missionaries of Charity constitutions is very clear and its spirit may be used as so many have done and are doing. Not to us, O Lord, not to us but to your name be glory!" Now its spirit is being made more broadly available to the many disciples of Mother Teresa throughout the world.

ONE

Our Call

You have not chosen me,
but I have chosen you. **Jn 15:16**

Let us make our society something
beautiful for God.

ℒ

HE HAS CHOSEN US; we have not first chosen him. But we must respond by making our society something beautiful for God—something very beautiful. For this we must give all—our utmost. We must cling to Jesus, grasp him, have a grip on him, and never let go for anything. We must fall in love with Jesus.

ℒ

Our particular mission is to labor at the salvation
and sanctification of the poorest of the poor not only in

the slums but all over the world, wherever they may be, by:

— *living the love of God in prayer and action in a life marked by the simplicity and humility of the gospel,*

— *loving Jesus under the appearance of bread,*

— *serving him in the distressing disguise of the poorest of the poor, both materially and spiritually, recognizing in them and restoring to them the image and likeness of God.*

As members of the active branch by:

— *nursing the sick and the dying destitutes,*

— *gathering and teaching little street children,*

— *visiting and caring for beggars, leprosy patients, and their children,*

— *giving shelter to the abandoned and homeless,*

— *caring for the unwanted, the unloved, and the lonely,*

— *going out to the spiritually poorest of the poor to proclaim the Word of God by our presence and spiritual works of mercy, and by,*

— *adoration of Jesus in the Blessed Sacrament.*

We are called the "Missionaries of Charity."

A missionary is one sent with a mission—a message to deliver. Just as Jesus was sent by his Father, we too are sent by him and filled with his Spirit to be witnesses of his gospel of love and compassion, first in our communities and then in our apostolate among the poorest of the poor all over the world.

As missionaries we must be:
— *carriers of God's love, ready to go in haste, like Mary—in search of souls,*
— *burning lights that give light to all men,*
— *the salt of the earth,*
— *souls consumed with one desire: Jesus. We must keep his interests continually in our hearts and minds, carrying our Lord to places where he has not walked before,*
— *fearless in doing the things he did, courageously going through danger and death with him and for him,*
— *ready to accept joyously the need to die daily if we want to bring souls to God, to pay the price he paid for souls,*
— *ever ready to go to any part of the world and to respect and appreciate unfamiliar customs of other peoples, their living conditions and language, willing to adapt ourselves if and when necessary,*
— *happy to undertake any labor and toil, and glad to make any sacrifice involved in our missionary life.*

"I THIRST"

"I thirst" Jesus said on the cross when he was deprived of every consolation and left alone, despised

and broken in body and soul.

As Missionaries of Charity we are called to quench this infinite thirst of a God made Man, who suffered, died, yet rose again and is now at the right hand of his Father making intercession for us:

— *by living the life of fervent charity in the practice of the four vows of chastity, poverty, obedience, and wholehearted free service to the poorest of the poor,*

— *by a deep life of prayer, contemplation, and penance,*

— *by accepting all suffering, renunciations, and even death,*

— *by being spouses of Jesus Crucified,*

ↆ

Hungry for love, he looks at you
Thirsty for kindness, he begs from you
Naked for loyalty, he hopes in you
Sick and imprisoned for friendship,
   he wants from you
Homeless for shelter in your heart,
   he asks of you.
Will you be that one to him?

ↆ

Each time anyone comes in contact with us, they must become different and better people because of having met us. We must radiate God's love.

꩜

"To quench the thirst of Jesus," for souls, means for love—for love of me and for love of others. When Jesus was dying on the cross, he cried, "I thirst." We have these words in every chapel of the Missionaries of Charity to remind us that a Missionary of Charity is here to quench the thirst of Jesus for souls, for love, for kindness, for compassion. When Jesus was in pain on the cross, the soldier, in order to help Jesus forget his pains, prepared the bitter drink of vinegar and gave it to him to drink. To avoid hurting the soldier, Jesus took it, but he only tasted it. He did not drink it because he did not want to forget the pain and the suffering. No . . . he loved me and he died for me . . . he suffered for me. Very often, we offer bitter drink to Jesus. This bitterness comes from the depth of our hearts and wells up in our words and our attitudes toward one another: "Whatever you do to the least of my brothers, you do it to me."

We have to quench the thirst of Jesus for others and for us. We do this by:

— nursing the sick and dying. By each action done to them I quench the thirst of Jesus for love of that person—by giving God's love in me to that particular person. How often we do not do that well!

— gathering and teaching little street children. I must give God's love to each of them and thus quench the thirst of Jesus.

— visiting and caring for beggars.

— giving shelter to the abandoned.

— caring for the unwanted, the unloved, the lonely—all the poor people.

This is how I quench the thirst of Jesus for others, by giving his love in action to them.

THE BREAD OF LIFE

As Missionaries of Charity we are especially called upon to see Christ in the appearance of bread and to touch him in the broken bodies of the poor.

Christ when he took bread said: "Take and eat, this is my body delivered for you." By giving himself, he invites us to grow in the power of his love to do what he has done.

Christ's love for us will give us strength and urge us to spend ourselves for him. "Let the sisters and the people eat you up." We have no right to refuse our life to others in whom we contact Christ.

Like Mary, let us be full of zeal to go in haste to give Jesus to others. She was full of grace when, at the annunciation, she received Jesus. Like her, we too become full of grace every time we receive Holy Communion. It is the same Jesus whom she received and whom we receive at Mass. As soon as she received him she went with haste to give him to John. For us also, as soon as we receive Jesus in Holy Communion, let us go in haste to give him to our sisters, to our poor, to the sick, to the dying, to the lepers, to the unwanted, and the unloved. By this we make Jesus present in the world today.

We cannot separate our lives from the Eucharist; the moment we do, something breaks. People ask, "Where do the sisters get the joy and energy to do what they are doing?" The Eucharist involves more than just receiving; it also involves satisfying the hunger of Christ. He says, "Come to me." He is hungry for souls. Nowhere does the Gospel say: "Go away," but always "come to me."

Our lives must be woven around the Eucharist. Ask Jesus to be with you, to work with you that you may be able to pray the work. You must really be sure that you have received Jesus. After that, you cannot give your tongue, your thoughts, or your heart to bitterness.

Put your sins in the chalice for the precious blood to wash away. One drop is capable of washing away all the sins of the world.

The Eucharist is connected with the passion. If Jesus had not established the Eucharist we would have forgotten the crucifixion. It would have faded into the past and we would have forgotten that Jesus loved us. There is a saying that to be far away from the eyes is to be far away from the heart. To make sure that we do not forget, Jesus gave us the Eucharist as a memorial of his love. To make sure that we keep on loving him, he gives us his hunger (to satisfy our hunger for him)—he gives us the poorest of the poor.

We must be faithful to that smallness of the Eucharist, that simple piece of bread which even a child can take in, that giving of a bath, that smile. . . . We have so much that we don't care about the small things. If we do not care, we will lose our grip on the Eucharist—on our lives. The Eucharist is so small.

I was giving Communion this morning. My two fingers were holding Jesus. Try to realize that Jesus allows himself to be broken. Make yourselves feel the need of each other. The passion and the Eucharist should open our eyes to that smallness: "This is my body; take and eat"—the small piece of bread. Today let us realize our own littleness in comparison with the Bread of Life.

❧

For us, we must never separate the Eucharist and the poor—or the poor and the Eucharist. You will really be a true Missionary of Charity when you go to the poor and take Jesus with you. He satisfied my hunger for him and now I go to satisfy his hunger for souls, for love.

❧

That is why Jesus made himself bread, to satisfy our hunger for God. See the humility of God. He also made himself the hungry one to satisfy our hunger for God through our love, our service. Let us pray that none of us will be unfaithful. Let us pray for our poor people. They are also hungry for God.

❧

Many years ago an angel came to bring the good news to Mary. The Prince of Peace was anxious to come to earth and an angel was used to bring the good news that the Creator would become a little child. The Prince of Peace was attracted to a young girl, who was a nobody in the eyes of the world. Even the angel could not understand why he was sent to a creature like that. But she was so beautiful that the King of Kings wanted to become flesh in her. She was so full of grace, so pure, so full of God. She looked at the angel—she must have been surprised for she had never seen an angel—and asked, how? What are you saying? I don't understand what you are saying; it makes no sense to me. And the angel said simply that by the power of the Holy Spirit, Christ would be formed within her. And Mary answered simply: "Behold the handmaid of the Lord."

In heaven everything was beautiful—yet, what attracted Jesus to the earth? The Son of God wanted to feel what it meant to be a human being; to be locked up for nine months, so dependent on a mother. That is why we say, "He, being rich, became poor"—so helpless!

When we recite the Creed we say "God from God, Light from Light." And there was the little body, so small. We find it so difficult to become small, and Jesus says to us: "Unless you become like little children you cannot enter the kingdom of God." And Mary knew and replied, "Yes, behold the handmaid of the Lord."

On the way to Addis Ababa, August 21, 1977

Now, more than ever we need to live out the teaching of Jesus: "Love one another, as the

Father has loved me." We have to love as the Father loves his Son Jesus, with the same mercy and compassion, joy and peace. Try to find out how the Father loves his Son, and then try to love one another in the same way. Find out in all humility how much you are loved by Jesus. From the time you realize that you are loved by Jesus, love as he loves you.

In each of our lives Jesus comes as the Bread of Life—to be eaten, to be consumed by us. That is how he loves us. He also comes as the Hungry One, hoping to be fed with the bread of our life, with our hearts that love and our hands that serve. In so doing, we prove that we have been created in the image and likeness of God, for God is love. When we love we are like God. This is what Jesus meant when he said: "Be perfect as your heavenly Father is perfect."

Jesus has chosen us for himself. We belong to him. Let us be so convinced of this "belonging" that we allow nothing, however small, to separate us from his love.

꙳

Motherhouse, August 29, 1980

That you may know each other at the breaking of the bread, love each other in the eating of the Bread of Life, and serve each other and him in his poor by giving whole-hearted service.

When communicating with Christ in your heart—the partaking of Living Bread—remember what Our Lady must have felt when the Spirit overpowered her and she, who was full of grace, became full with the body of Jesus. The Spirit in her was so strong that she immediately rose in haste to go and serve.

Each Holy Communion, each breaking of the Bread of Life, each sharing should produce in us the same, for it is the same Jesus who came to Mary and was made flesh. We, too, should be in haste to give this life of Jesus to our sisters and the poor.

WE ARE CHOSEN

"I will betroth you to me forever in steadfast love, in mercy. I will betroth you to me in faithfulness" (Hos 19:20).

Thank God from the depths of your heart that he has chosen you for himself and for life.

What is our vocation? What do we call vocation? Our vocation is Jesus. We have it in the Scripture very clearly: "I have called you by name, you are precious to me . . . I have called you my friend. Water will not drown you."

(Water symbolizes all the temptations of evil.) "I will give nations for you; you are precious." "How could a mother forget her child? Or a woman the child within her womb? But even if a mother could forget, I will never forget you. You are precious to me; you are carved in the palm of my hand."

Why are we here? We must have heard Jesus calling us by name. We are like St. Paul. Once he realized the love of Christ, he cared about nothing else. He did not care whether he was scourged or put into prison. For him, only one thing was important: Jesus Christ.

ॐ

God loves me. I'm not here just to fill a place, just to be a number. He has chosen me for a purpose. I know it. He will fulfill it if I don't put an obstacle in his way. He will not force me. God could have forced Our Lady. Jesus could have come just like that. The Holy Spirit could have come. But God wanted Mary to say yes. It is the same with us. God doesn't force us, but he wants us to say yes.

God doesn't want one more congregation in the world—just three thousand nuns more. We have been created and chosen to proclaim his love so that people may see the wonderful works of God. I will never forget a man in

Kalighat who observed a sister as she was taking care of a patient. The sister did not know she was being watched. Afterwards the man came to me and said: "Mother, I came here godless. Today I found God in that sister—the way she was looking at the sick person and taking care of him." This is what we have been created for—to proclaim Christ's love, to proclaim his presence.

CALLED TO BE SAINTS

"I am the Vine and my Father is the Vinedresser. Every branch that bears fruit he prunes that it may bear more fruit" (Jn 15:1-2).

I will give saints to Mother Church!

℞

Let us live the life of union with God. All our little actions may be offered through the precious blood—through Jesus. We have learned that. Let us never be satisfied. Jesus poured out every drop of blood, not just some of it. Let us do the same. We have to learn to become virtuous. We must be full of holy ambition to be the holiest sister.

℞

God said to one of our sisters: "I have so many sisters like you—ordinary, good sisters; I can pave the streets with them. I want fervent ones: saints. 'I looked for one to comfort me and I found none.'"

There is so much unhappiness, so much misery everywhere. Our human nature stays with us from beginning to end. We must work hard every day to conquer ourselves. We must learn to be meek and humble of heart. Let us try to give everything to Jesus: every word, every moment. Jesus, use my eyes, my ears, my feet! My resolution must be firm: to become a saint.

Jesus said, "Learn of me." In our meditations we should always say, "Jesus, make me a saint according to your own heart, meek and humble." We must respond in the spirit in which Jesus meant us to respond. We know him better now, through meditations, and the study of the gospel, but have we really understood him in his humility? Does this humility appeal to us, attract us? Humility is nothing but truth. What have we got that we have not received? asks St. Paul. If I have not received anything, what good have I on my own?

℧

If you are humble, nothing will touch you, neither praise nor disgrace, because you know what you are. If you are blamed, you won't be discouraged; if anyone calls you a saint, you won't put yourself on a pedestal. If you are a saint, thank God; if you are a sinner don't remain one. Christ tells us to aim very high, not to be like Abraham or David or any of the saints, but to be like our heavenly Father.

ॱ

The more repugnant the work the greater should be our faith and cheerful devotion. That we feel repugnance is but natural, but when we overcome it for love of Jesus we may become heroic. Very often it has happened in the lives of the saints that a heroic overcoming of repugnance has been what has lifted them to sanctity.

This was the case with St. Francis of Assisi, who, when meeting a completely disfigured leper, drew back. But then, overcoming himself, he kissed the terrible, disfigured face. The result was that Francis was filled with an untold joy. He became the complete master of himself, and the leper walked away praising God for his cure.

ॱ

Self-knowledge puts us on our knees and it is very necessary for love. For knowledge of God produces love, and knowledge of self produces humility. Self-knowledge is a very important thing in our lives. As St. Augustine says, "Fill yourselves first, and then only will you be able to give to others." Self-knowledge is also a safeguard against pride, especially when one is tempted later in life. The greatest mistake is to think one is too strong to fall into temptation. Put your finger in the fire and it will burn. Don't play with temptation.

Holiness is not the luxury of the few. It is a simple duty for each one of us, especially for us who have been chosen. We have been chosen to belong to Christ.

ℚ

First Friday in October 1960

The first step "to becoming" is to will it. St. Thomas says that "sanctity consists in nothing else than a firm resolution, the heroic act of a soul abandoning herself to God." By an upright will we love God, we run towards God, we reach him, we possess him.

"O good, good will which transforms me into the image of God and makes me like to him," so St. Augustine says. My progress in holiness depends on God and myself: on God's grace and my will.

We must have a real, living resolution to reach holiness. St. Teresa says that Satan is terribly afraid of resolute souls. Everything depends on these two or three words: "I will" or

"I will not." I must put all my energy into this "will." St. John Berchmans, St. Stanislaus, St. Margaret Mary said "I will," and they did become saints. What is a saint but simply a resolute soul, a soul that uses power plus action? Wasn't this what St. Paul meant when he said: "I can do all things in Him who strengthens me?" My sisters, I will not be satisfied if you are just good religious. I want to be able to offer God a perfect sacrifice. Only holiness perfects the gift.

"To resolve to be a saint" means I will despoil myself of all that is not God: I will strip my heart and empty it of all created things: I will live in poverty and detachment. I will renounce my will, my inclinations, my whims and fancies and offer myself as a willing slave to the will of God. Yes, my children, this is what I pray for daily, for each one, that you may become a slave to the will of God.

ҁ

Rome, October 8, 1980

Holiness is the main reason for the existence of our society. For us, holiness should not be difficult—for in giving wholehearted free service to the poorest of the poor, we are with Jesus twenty-four hours. And, since every Missionary of Charity is the poorest of the poor, we live and observe the fourth vow even when we do small things for each other.

Nothing can make me holy except the presence of God and to me the presence of God is fidelity to small things. Fidelity to small things will lead you to Christ. Infidelity to small things will lead you to sin.

TWO

Our Response

*Father, into your hands I commend
    my spirit.* **Lk 23:46**

*A Missionary of Charity must be a
Missionary of Charity of joy. By this
sign the world will know you are
Missionaries of Charity.*

ↄ

*The spirit of our society is one of total surrender, loving
trust and cheerfulness, as lived by Jesus and Mary in
the Gospel.*

TOTAL SURRENDER

Our total surrender to God means to be entirely at
the disposal of the Father as Jesus and Mary were. In
giving ourselves completely to God, because God has

given himself to us, we are entirely at his disposal,

> *— to be possessed by him so that we may possess him,*
>
> *— to take whatever he gives and to give whatever he takes with a big smile,*
>
> *— to be used by him as it pleases him without being consulted,*
>
> *— to offer him our free will, our reason, our whole life in pure faith, so that he may think his thoughts in our minds, do his work through our hands, and love with our hearts.*

❧

Total surrender consists in giving ourselves completely to God. Why must we give ourselves fully to God? Because God has given himself to us. If God, who owes nothing to us, is ready to impart to us no less than himself, shall we answer with just a fraction of ourselves? To give ourselves fully to God is a means of receiving God himself. I live for God and give up my own self and in this way induce God to live for me. Therefore, to possess God, we must allow him to possess our souls. How poor we would be if God had not given us the power of giving ourselves to him. How rich we are now. How easy it is to conquer God! We give ourselves to God; then God is ours and there can be nothing more ours than God. The money with which God repays our surrender is himself.

❧

Our total surrender will come today by surrendering even our sins so that we will be poor. "Unless you become a child you cannot come to me." You are too big, too heavy; you cannot be lifted up. We need humility to acknowledge our sin. The knowledge of our sin helps us to rise. I will get up and go to my Father.

❧

It must have been so hard to have been scourged, to have been spat upon. "Take it away," Jesus prayed during his agony. His Father didn't come to him directly and say, "This is my beloved Son," but he consoled him through an angel. Let us pray that we will fill our hearts with Jesus' surrender, that we will understand total surrender.

We should not be concerned with the instrument God uses to speak to us, whether the pencil writes in blue ink or green, but with what God is saying to us. Let us pray to understand what it means to be at his disposal.

❧

God's tender love for us is great. We receive so much. People give to us so abundantly. Our answer to God for his tremendous love is total surrender. . . . he can do with us whatever he wants. Once the Cardinal of St. Louis asked me to write something for him in his breviary. I wrote, "Let Jesus use you without consulting you." He wrote back, "You don't know what you have done to me. I examine my conscience every day and ask, 'Did I allow Jesus to use me without consulting me?' "

॥

Our vocation is the conviction that "I belong to him." Because I belong to him, he must be free to use me. I must surrender completely. When we look at his cross, we understand his love. His head is bent down to kiss us. His hands are extended to embrace us. His heart is wide open to receive us. This is what we have to be in the world today. We, too, must have our head bent down to our people—to the school where we are teaching or to the sick and dying destitute that we are helping. This is Jesus in his distressing disguise. Whether in the school or in the slum, it is the same Jesus. He said very clearly, "You did it to me. I was hungry . . . I was naked . . . I was homeless." Let us not make the mistake of thinking that the hunger is only for a piece of bread. The hunger of today is much greater; it is a hunger for love, to be wanted, to be cared for, to be somebody.

There is such a beautiful thing in India—the red dot on the forehead. The meaning for the Hindu is that his whole thought and attention, everything must be concentrated on God. For the married woman it is the same. The red marking along the part in her hair means that all her thoughts are for her husband. We, too, must be fully for Jesus, giving him that undivided love.

LOVING TRUST

One thing Jesus asks of me: that I lean on him; that in him and only in him I put complete trust; that I surrender myself to him unreservedly. Even when all goes wrong and I feel as if I am a ship without a compass, I must give myself completely to him. I must not attempt to control God's action; I must not count the stages in the journey he would have me make. I must not desire a clear perception of my advance upon the road, must not know precisely where I am upon the way of holiness. I ask him to make a saint of me, yet I must leave to him the choice of the saintliness itself and still more the means which leads to it.

❧

We need to trust our poor people. The greatest injustice done to our poor is that we fail to trust them, to respect them, to love them. How often we just push and pull.

❧

Total surrender involves loving trust. You cannot surrender totally unless you trust lovingly and totally. Jesus trusted his Father because he knew him, he knew of his love. "My Father and I are one." "The Father is in me and I am in the Father." "I am not alone, the Father is with me." "Father, into your hands I commend my Spirit." Read St. John's Gospel and see how many times Jesus used the word "Father." Jesus came to reveal the Father. In the time of the Old Testament God was known as the God of fear, punishment, and anger. The coming of Jesus reverses this picture completely. God in the New Testament is the God of love, compassion, and mercy. That is why we can trust him fully—there is no more fear. This loving trust implies that we know the love of God and that we proclaim this love, compassion, and mercy everywhere we are sent. Today we reveal him.

God will never, never, never let us down if we have faith and put our trust in him. For the very first time one week we had no rice to give the people. We were feeding four thousand people each day and these were people who simply would not eat unless the sisters fed them. But we had nothing. Then, about nine in the morning on Friday, two truckloads full of bread arrived. It was more bread than these people had ever seen in their lives.

The schools had been closed unexpectedly and the bread that would have been used in the schools that day was sent to the sisters. So, you see, God is thoughtful. He will never let us down if we trust him, even if he has to play a trick on people and close down the schools. He will always look after us. So we must cleave to Jesus. Our whole life must simply be woven into Jesus. Jesus in the Mass, Jesus in my sisters, in the poor, at adoration. It is the same Jesus. Just as the wine and the grape are one; just as the branch fits so tightly into the vine—so we must be completely one with Jesus.

CHEERFULNESS

Joy is indeed the fruit of the Holy Spirit and a characteristic mark of the kingdom of God, for God is Joy.

Christ wanted to share his joy with his apostles "That my joy may be in you, and that your joy may be full" (Jn 15:11).

Joy is prayer,
  — *the sign of our generosity, selflessness, and close and continual union with God.*

Joy is love,
  — *a joyful heart is the normal result of a heart burning with love, for she gives most who gives with joy, and God loves a cheerful giver.*

Joy is a net of love by which we can catch souls,
  — *a sister filled with joy preaches without preaching. Joy is a need and a power for us even physically, for it makes us always ready to go about doing good.*

The joy of the Lord is our strength.

ॐ

Persuaded of our nothingness and with the blessing of obedience we attempt all things, doubting nothing, for with God all things are possible. We will allow the good God to make plans for the future, for yesterday has gone, tomorrow has not yet come, and we have only today to make him known, loved, and served. Grateful for the thousands of opportunities Jesus gives us to bring hope into a multitude of lives by our concern for the individual sufferer, we will help our troubled world at the brink of despair to discover a new reason to live or to die with a smile of contentment on its lips.

꒰

We do not allow ourselves to be disheartened by any failure as long as we have done our best, neither do we glory in our success but refer all to God in deepest thankfulness.

With Jesus our Savior, "the Lamb led to the slaughter," and with our poor, we will accept cheerfully and in the spirit of faith, all the opportunities he makes especially for us—those of misunderstanding, of being looked down on, of failure, disgrace, blame, lack of virtue, and correction.

꒰

Like Jesus, who submitted himself to the common law of labor and the common lot of the poor, we will:

— not seek any special privileges or treatment for ourselves, but be happy to be treated as one of the poor, ready to be insulted, ill-treated, refused, blamed falsely, or put to all kinds of inconveniences. We shall not seek to defend ourselves, but leave our defense to the Lord.

— not worry about tomorrow but will live the present moment intensely, with complete trust in God.

— *Joyfully and with eagerness, fearlessly and openly, giving freely what we have freely received, without accepting any return in cash or kind, reward or gratitude.*

~

Cheerfulness should be one of the main points of our religious life. A cheerful giver is a great giver. Cheerfulness is a sign of a generous and mortified person, who, forgetting all things, even herself, tries to please God in all she does for souls. Cheerfulness is often a cloak which hides a life of sacrifice, continual union with God, fervor, and generosity.

~

Joy is one of the most essential things in our Society. A Missionary of Charity must be a Missionary of Charity of joy. She must radiate that joy to everyone. By this sign the world will know you are Missionaries of Charity. Everyone in the world sees you and remarks and speaks out about the Missionaries of Charity, not because of what they do but because they are happy to do the work they do and live the life they live. "That my joy may be in you," says Jesus. What is this joy of Jesus? It is the result of his continual union with God, doing the will of the Father. This joy is the fruit of union with

God, of being in the presence of God. Living in the presence of God fills us with joy. God is joy. To bring joy to us, Jesus became man. Mary was the first one to receive Jesus: "My spirit rejoices in God my Savior." The child in Elizabeth's womb leapt with joy because Mary carried Jesus to him.

In Bethlehem, joy filled everyone: the shepherds, the angels, the three kings, Joseph, and Mary. Joy was also the characteristic mark of the first Christians. During the persecution, people used to look for those who had this joy radiating on their faces. By that joy, they knew who the Christians were and thus they persecuted them. St. Paul, whom we are trying to imitate in our zeal, was an apostle of joy. He urged the early Christians to rejoice in the Lord always. Paul's whole life can be summed up in one sentence, "I belong to Christ." Nothing can separate me from the Love of Christ, neither suffering nor persecution nor anything. "I live, now it is no longer I who live but it is Christ who lives in me." That is why St. Paul was so full of joy.

Joy is love, the normal result of a heart burning with love. Our lamp will be burning with sacrifices made out of love if we have joy. Then the Bridegroom will say, "Come and possess the kingdom prepared for you." It is a joyful sister who gives most. Everyone loves the one who gives with joy and so does God. Don't we always turn to someone who will give happily and without grumbling? "Joy is a net of love by which we catch souls." Because we are full of joy, everyone wants to be with us and to receive the light of Christ that we possess. A sister filled with joy preaches without preaching. Daily, we pray, "Help me to spread your fragrance," yours, Lord, not mine. Do we realize its meaning? Do we realize our mission of spreading this joy, of radiating this joy daily as we go about our lives?

April 1964

Joy is not simply a matter of temperament. In the service of God and souls, it is always hard to be joyful—all the more reason why we should try to acquire it and make it grow in our hearts.

Joy is prayer; joy is strength; joy is love; joy is a net of love by which we catch souls. God loves a cheerful giver. She gives most who gives with joy. If in the work you have difficulties and you accept them with joy, with a big smile—in this like in any other thing—they will see your good works and glorify the Father. The best way to show your gratitude is to accept everything with joy. A joyful heart is the normal result of a heart burning with love.

Joy is a need and a power for us, even physically. A sister who has cultivated a spirit of joy feels less tired and is always ready to go on doing good. Joy is one of the best safeguards against temptations. The devil is a carrier of dust and dirt—he uses every chance to throw what he has at us. A joyful heart knows how to protect itself from such dirt: Jesus can take full possession of our soul only if it surrenders itself joyfully. St. Teresa was worried about her sisters only when she saw any of them lose their joy. God is joy. He is love. A sister filled with joy preaches without preaching. A joyful sister is like the sunshine of God's love, the hope of eternal happiness, the flame of burning love.

In our society, a cheerful disposition is one of the main virtues required for a Missionary of Charity. The spirit of our society is total surrender, loving trust, and cheerfulness. That is why the society expects us to accept humiliations readily and with joy; to live the life of poverty with cheerful trust; to imitate the chastity of Mary, the cause of our joy; to offer cheerful obedience from inward joy; to minister to Christ in his distressing disguise with cheerful devotion.

MISSIONARIES OF LOVE

We must not be ashamed to love Christ with our emotions. A woman loves her husband with her whole heart. In her autobiography, the Little Flower tells about a relative who came to see her. This woman was always talking about her husband, about his long hair, his beautiful eyes, and so on. She expressed her love for him so beautifully. The Little Flower listened to her and then wrote these words in her diary: "I will never allow a woman to love her husband more than I love you, O Jesus Christ."

Jesus was everything to her. She was so attached to Christ. Is it the same for you? Do you love Christ like that? We must love Christ with our emotions. We are all women. Let us all make use of our ability to love.

Be one with him, joined to him and united to him so that nothing, absolutely nothing, can separate you from the love of Christ. He belongs to you and you belong to him. It's as simple as that. Accept whatever he gives and give whatever he takes with a big smile.

Yet, we forget. We can love the leper, the one with the broken and disfigured face, but we forget to love our sister when she is proud or impatient. We forget that it is only a distressing disguise, that the person is really Jesus. We do not have undivided love for Christ but, instead, we let the devil trick us with the distressing disguise. We must be holy. We must be able to see Jesus in our sisters and in the poor.

༄

When the Little Flower was canonized, no great things were uncovered for her canonization. She was canonized for one thing only. As Pius X said, "She did ordinary things with extraordinary love"—small things with great love. This is what you and I gave when we gave our word to Jesus. This is our vow.

༄

"A Missionary of Charity *must be a missionary of love.*" A missionary is one who is sent. God sent his Son. Today God sends us. Each one of us is sent by God. Why are we sent? We are sent to be his love among men, to bring his love and compassion to the poorest of the poor. We must not be afraid to love. A Missionary of Charity *must* be a missionary of love. Notice the words *"must be."* It is not that she should simply try to be. No, she *must be* a missionary of love. She is sent to *be* God's love.

༄

Even Almighty God cannot fill what is already full. We must be empty if we want God to fill us with his fullness. Our Lady had to be empty before she could be full of grace. She had to declare that she was the handmaid of the Lord before God could fill her. So also we must be empty of all pride, all jealousy, of all selfishness before God can fill us with his love.

We must be able to give ourselves so completely to God that he must be able to possess us. We must "Give whatever he takes and take whatever he gives."

How unlike him we are. How little love, how little compassion, how little forgiveness, how little kindness we have. We are not worthy to be so close to him—to enter his heart. For his heart is still open to embrace us. His head is still crowned with thorns, his hands nailed to the cross today. Let us find out: "Are the nails mine? That spit on his face, is it mine? What part of his body, of his mind, has suffered because of me?" We should ask, not with anxiety or fear, but with a meek and humble heart. Let us find out what part of his body has wounds inflicted by our sin. Let us not go alone but put our hands in his. He is there to forgive seventy times seven. Our Father loves us. He has called us in a special way, given us a name. We belong to him with all our misery, our sin, our weakness, our goodness. We are his.

Let us not be like the rich young man in the Gospel. Jesus saw him and loved him and wanted him but he had given his heart to something else—to his riches. He was rich, young, and strong. Jesus could not fill him. Instead, be like Zacchaeus. He was a little man—a small man—and he knew his smallness. He recognized his smallness and made a very simple decision in order to see Jesus. He climbed a tree because he knew he was small. If he hadn't opened his heart and responded to Jesus in that simple way, Jesus could not have shown his love, he could not have said, "Come down, Zacchaeus! Come down!" This is the foundation of everything: "Learn of me, that I am meek and humble of heart." Be small.

If my love for my sisters is okay, then my love for Jesus will be okay. There are not two loves. The deeper my love for Jesus, the deeper that love for my sisters, the greater the zeal to go to the poor.

THREE

Our Way of Life

I am the Way, the Truth, and the Life.
Jn 14:16

Just as the seed is meant to be a tree—
we are meant to grow into Jesus.

ॐ

Each of us will accept:
— to live the life of poverty in cheerful trust
— to imitate the chastity of Mary, the cause of
  our joy
— to offer cheerful obedience from inward
  joy.

POVERTY

*"The foxes have holes and the birds of the air have
nests but the Son of Man has nowhere to lay his head"*
(Lk 9:5-7).

Our poverty is our dowry.

With regard to God, our poverty is our humble recognition and acceptance of our sinfulness, helplessness, and utter nothingness, and the acknowledgement of our neediness before him, which expresses itself as hope in him, as an openness to receive all things from him as from our Father.

Our poverty should be true gospel poverty—gentle, tender, glad, and openhearted, always ready to give an expression of love. Poverty is love before it is renunciation. To love, it is necessary to give. To give, it is necessary to be free from selfishness.

❧

Desirous to share Christ's own poverty and that of our poor:

— We accept to have everything in common and to share with one another in the Society.

— We do not accept anything whatsoever from our parents, friends, or benefactors for our personal use. Whatever is given to us is handed over to our superiors for the common use of the community or for the work.

— We shall eat the food of the people, of the country where we live, using what is cheapest. It should be sufficient and wholesome so as to maintain good health which is essential for the work of our vocation.

— *Our houses should be simple and modest, places where the poor feel at home.*

— *We shall walk whenever opportunity offers, in order to take the cheapest means of transport available.*

— *We shall sleep in common dormitories without privacy like the poor.*

— *We and our poor will depend entirely on Divine Providence both for our material and spiritual needs.*

ॽ

Whenever it is necessary, we will do our begging willingly, in the spirit of poverty and cheerful trust— becoming beggars for the poor members of Christ who himself lived on alms during his public life and whom we serve in the sick and the poor. We shall not store things nor shall we beg for more than what is necessary.

ॽ

In our society we must try to aim at a most perfect poverty. It is to be a wall of defense which has two effects:

— It excludes the enemy. As we know from the Spiritual Exercises, the first trick of the devil is to lead men to the love of wealth; the true love of evangelical poverty closes this avenue of our soul to the evil spirit.

—It secures peace and protection for those
who dwell within the wall.

ॐ

Our Lord on the cross possessed nothing. He
was on the cross which was given by Pilate. The
nails and the crown were given him by the
soldiers. He was naked, and when he died,
cross, nails, and crown were taken away from
him. And he was wrapped in a shroud given
him by a kind man and buried in a tomb which
was not his.

ॐ

We must never get into the habit of being
preoccupied with the future. There is no reason
to do so. God is there. Once the longing for
money comes, the longing also comes for what
money can give: superfluities, nice rooms,
luxuries at table, more clothes, fans, etc. Our
needs will increase, for one thing brings another
and the result will be endless dissatisfaction.

Poverty makes us free. That is why we can
joke and smile and keep a happy heart for Jesus.

The first true poverty was when "Christ
emptied himself." For nine months he was lost
in the little space of Mary's bosom: not even St.
Joseph knew who he was. Having all things, yet
possessing nothing. His birth was also like one
of the poorest of the poor. Even our poor have

someone to assist them . . . Mary did not. At Nazareth even his people despised him. It was not necessary for Jesus to practice this absolute poverty. There is only one reason: because he desired it. He wanted to be to the fullest "one" of us.

✎

Poverty is necessary because we are working with the poor. When they complain about the food, we can say: we eat the same. They say, "It was so hot last night, we could not sleep." We can reply, "We also felt very hot." The poor have to wash for themselves, go barefoot; we do the same. We have to go down and lift them up. It opens the heart of the poor when we can say we live the same way they do. Sometimes they only have one bucket of water. It is the same with us. The poor have to stand in line; we do too. Food, clothing, everything must be like that of the poor. We have no fasting. Our fasting is to eat the food as we get it.

✎

Christ being rich emptied himself. This is where contradiction lies. If I want to be poor like Christ—who became poor even though he was rich—I must do the same. Nowadays people want to be poor and live with the poor, but they want to be free to dispose of things as they wish. To have this freedom is to be rich. They want both and they cannot have both. This is another kind of contradiction.

Our poverty is our freedom. This is our poverty—the giving up of our freedom to dispose of things, to choose, to possess. The moment I use and dispose of things as mine, that moment I cease to be poor.

We must strive to acquire the true spirit of poverty which manifests itself in a love for the practice of the virtue of poverty in imitation of Christ—in imitation of him who chose it as the companion of his life on earth when he came to live among us. Christ did not have to lead a life of poverty. Thus he taught us how important it is for our sanctification.

We practice the virtue of poverty when we mend our clothes quickly and as beautifully as we can. To go about in a torn habit and sari is certainly not the sign of the virtue of poverty. For, remember, we do not profess the poverty of beggars, but the poverty of Christ. Let us also remember that our body is the temple of the Holy Spirit, and for that reason we must respect it always with neatly mended clothes. We would never dream of using dirty, torn cloth as a tabernacle veil to cover the door of the dwelling that Christ chose for himself on earth since his Ascension into heaven. In the same way, we should never cover the temple of the Holy Spirit, which is our body, with torn, dirty, untidy clothes. Patched clothes are no disgrace. It is said of St. Francis of Assisi that when he died his habit had so many patches that the original cloth was no longer there.

※

The poor are great people and we owe them deep gratitude, for if they did not accept us then we would not exist as Missionaries of Charity. To be able to understand this, we look at Jesus. To be able to become man, he, being rich, became poor. He could have chosen the king's palace, but to be equal to us, he chose to be like us in all things except sin. To be equal to the poor, we choose to be poor like them in everything except destitution. Each of us has given our word to God to follow Christ in poverty.

※

When you make the vow of poverty, you say "I have nothing." That is why you cannot destroy things or give them away without permission. By right, you can't even say, "This is my sari." For us, poverty is freedom. You are free to love God—free to love Jesus with an undivided heart.

The devil is very busy. The more our work involves bringing souls to God, the more he tries to take us away from God, to spoil the work. Poverty provides tremendous protection. I call it freedom. Nothing and nobody will separate me from the love of Christ.

You must experience the joy of poverty. Poverty is not only renunciation. Poverty is joy. Poverty is love. My reason for doing without is that "I love Jesus." Unless you experience for yourself this joy of poverty, you will never understand what I am saying. Have the courage to live that poverty. Jesus was born in Bethlehem. All he had was a piece of cloth, some straw. Picture the animals gathering around the child. There were no electric heaters. Our Lady must have taught him to walk. He could have come down from heaven as a full grown man, but he came to us as an infant. Everything had to be done for him. He became poor for love of us.

I will never forget something that happened when I was at Loreto. One of the children was very, very naughty. She was only six or seven years old. One day, when she was extremely naughty, I took her hand and said, "Come, we're going for a walk." She had some money with her. One hand held my hand and the other held tightly to the money. "I will buy this, I will buy that," she kept saying. Suddenly she saw a blind beggar, and at once she left the money with him. From that day she was a completely different child. She was so small and so naughty. Yet that one decision changed her life. It is the same with you. Get rid of anything that's holding you back. If you want to be all for Jesus, the decision has to come from within you.

ᴥ

I want you to experience that joy of poverty which is really the perfect joy of St. Francis of Assisi. He called it Lady Poverty. St. Ignatius called it Mother Poverty. The more we have, the less we can give. So let us have less to be able to give all to Jesus.

ᴥ

Motherhouse, March 22, 1981

As our poor keep growing in poverty—due to the great rise in the cost of living—let us be more careful regarding the poverty of our houses. The daily needs that our poor cannot get—let us be more careful in the use of them—

so that we also feel the hardship in food, clothing, water, electricity, soap—things which our poor often go without.

CHASTITY

Our vow of chastity is our response to the call of Christ. Our vow is made to God alone by which we commit ourselves:
  — *to live a celibate life in the fervor of charity and the perfection of chastity, for we are convinced that complete continence is neither impossible nor harmful to human development because, in the maturity and delicacy of our vocation as women, we love Christ with a deep and personal love, expressed in our love for our sisters, our poor, and the world in which we live.*
  — *in a spirit of renunciation, not only to renounce marriage but also to engage ourselves to avoid every external or internal offense against chastity.*

Our vow of chastity liberates us totally for the contemplation of God and the wholehearted and free service of the poorest of the poor. By it we cleave to Jesus with undivided love so as to:
  — *live in him, for him, by him, and with him as our sole guide,*

> — *be invaded by his own holiness and filled with his own Spirit of love,*
> — *show forth the luminous face of Jesus, radiant with purity and love for the Father and mankind,*
> — *make reparation to God for all the sins of the flesh committed in the world today.*

ℛ

By our vow of chastity we do renounce God's natural gift to women to become mothers—for the greater gift—that of being virgins for Christ, of entering into a much more beautiful motherhood.

ℛ

One day at a meeting, I was asked to give a message. So I told the people, "Husbands smile at your wives; wives smiles at your husbands and your children." They could not understand how I was able to tell them this sort of thing. "Are you married?" one of them asked. "Yes," I replied, "and sometimes I find it difficult to smile at Jesus because he can be so demanding." And it is true. By our vow of chastity we are married to Jesus.

ℛ

In my heart there is only one vacant seat. It is for God and nobody else. Temptation is like fire in which gold is purified. So we have to go through this fire. The temptations are allowed by God. The only thing we have to do is to refuse to give in. If I say I do not want it, I am safe. There may be temptations against purity, against faith , against my vocation. If we love our vocation, we will be tempted. But then we will also grow in sanctity. We have to fight temptation for the love of God.

❧

By the vow of chastity, I not only renounce the married state of life, but I also consecrate to God the free use of my internal and external acts—my affections. I cannot in conscience love a creature with the love of a woman for a man. I no longer have the right to give that affection to any other creature but only to God.

What, then? Do we have to be stones, human beings without hearts? Do we simply say: "I don't care; to me all human beings are the same." No, not at all. We have to keep ourselves as we are, but keep it all for God, to whom we have consecrated all our external and internal acts.

❧

Our Lord, at his dying moment, thought of his mother. That is the proof that he was human to the last. Therefore, if you have a loving nature, keep it and use it for God; if you have a genial temperament that causes you to smile, keep it and use it for God.

People in the world think that the vow of chastity makes us inhuman, makes us become like stones, without feelings. Each one of us can tell them it is not true. It is the vow of chastity that gives us the freedom to love everybody instead of simply becoming a mother to three or four children. A married woman can love but one man; we can love the whole world in God. The vow of chastity does not diminish us; it makes us live to the full if it is kept properly. The vow of chastity is not simply a list of don'ts—it is love. I give myself to God and I receive God. God becomes my own and I become his own. That is why I become completely dedicated to him by the vow of chastity.

God does not want to impose a burden on us by the vow of chastity. We must love our consecration, which sets us apart for God alone. We must be free of things to be full of God. The vow of chastity sets us free to love with our whole heart and soul for God's sake.

By my vow of chastity I free myself for the kingdom of God. I become his property and he binds himself to take care of me. I must then give wholehearted free service. What is this wholehearted free service? It is the outcome of chastity, of binding myself to Christ. Therefore, I bind myself to give not half-hearted but wholehearted service. When we neglect to do our work well, this vow suffers most—our service to the poor—because we become preoccupied with whatever we are giving our affection to.

༚

Don't allow anything to interfere with your love for Jesus. You belong to him. *Nothing can separate you from him.* That one sentence is important to remember. He will be your joy, your strength. If you hold onto that sentence, temptations and difficulties will come, but nothing will break you.

༚

Receive the symbol of our crucified spouse. I have chosen to be the spouse of Jesus crucified. Follow his footsteps in search of souls by showing great love in small things. He comes down to proclaim the good news to the poor through our works of love. We are Missionaries of Charity for that one reason only. Carry him and his light into the homes of the poor.

༚

"Remember always, beloved daughters in Christ, the value of your religious consecration.

Through your consecration to the Lord Jesus you respond to his love and discover the needs of his brothers and sisters throughout the world. This consecration, expressed through your vows, is the source of your joy and fulfillment. It is the secret of your supernatural contribution to the kingdom of God. It is the measure of the effectiveness of your service to the poor, the guarantee that it will last.

"Yes, to belong to Christ Jesus is a great gift of God's love, and may the world always see this love in your smile. To all of you goes our Apostolic Blessing" (Pope Paul VI, Rome, June 5, 1978).

These are the Holy Father's last words to the Missionaries of Charity. Go to Jesus and repeat to him what I've told you. "Jesus in my heart, I love you. I believe in your love for me."

ꝟ

Chastity does not simply mean that we are not married. It means that we love Christ with an undivided love. To be pure we need poverty. Is it wrong to have things? We vow poverty not because it is wrong to have things but we choose to do without these things.

ꝟ

The vow of chastity is to love Christ with undivided, loving chastity. It is not only that we cannot have a family, we cannot get married.

But it is something deeper, something living, something real—it is to love him with undivided, loving chastity through the freedom of poverty. We must be free to love—and to love him with an undivided love. Nothing will separate us from the love of Christ—and that is our vow of chastity.

By this vow we are bound to remain faithful to the humble works of the society: to the poorest of the poor, the unwanted, the unloved, the uncared for. That means we depend solely on Divine Providence. After years of dealing with thousands and thousands of people, we have never yet had to send anybody away because we didn't have something to give them. There has always been one more plate of rice, one more bed. We have never had to say, "I'm sorry, I cannot take you in or I cannot give you anything."

I remember when I was leaving home fifty years ago—my mother was dead set against me leaving home and becoming a sister. In the end, when she realized that this was what God wanted from her and from me, she said something very strange: "Put your hand in his hand and walk all alone with him." This is exactly our way of life. We may be surrounded by many people, yet our vocation is really lived out alone with Jesus.

◌

What am I binding myself to? What is my vow to God about?—I bind myself to God with undivided love. I tell Almighty God, "I can love all, but the only one I *will* love in particular is you, only you."

◌

To be able to understand chastity we must know what poverty and obedience are. They are like the pillars. If we remove the pillars, the whole building will tip to one side and fall.

OBEDIENCE

"Behold I come to do your will, O God" (Heb 12:7).
Submission for someone who is in love is more than a duty—it is a blessedness.
Jesus, only Begotten Son of the Father, equal to his Father, God from God, Light from Light, did not feel it below his dignity to obey.
Therefore, we will:
— accept, love, and respect all our lawful superiors,
— sincerely pray for them,
— show joyful trust in, and loyalty to them,
— make our obedience cheerful, prompt, simple,

and constant without question or excuse.

We should obey the known wish of our superiors as well as their commands in a spirit of faith. They may make a mistake in commanding, but we are infallible in obeying.

❧

Whenever our superiors think it desirable for the greater glory of God to give us a change of residence, work, or companions, we should welcome this change as the very will of God and show a humble and joyful obedience.

❧

Let the superior remember that she is first for the sisters and next for the work. Therefore, let all her dealings with her sisters be motherly, never discouraging them, especially when they fail. Let her take special care of the old and the sick and of those who do not take due care of themselves. In the house work let her be always the first to put her hand to the work. Let her have nothing special or different in food, clothes, or lodging. Let her trust her sisters completely. Let her be generous when the sisters observe poverty fervently. Let her house be a house of love, joy, and peace.

❧

True obedience is a genuine act of love. Obedience makes us practice the other virtues.

It likens us to martyrs, for it is a much greater martyrdom to persevere in obedience all through life than to die in a moment by a stroke of the sword.

꿎

The superior is in the place of God. The position given to her is like a chair. The chair remains, but the person can change. Today I sit in the chair; tomorrow somebody else might be sitting there. But the chair is the same. The chair may not fit some as well as others. Some are too short for it and others too tall, while yet others fit it perfectly. The chair is in the place of God who gave your superior this position. I have to obey if I want to go on in peace.

꿎

It is impossible that a sister who is obedient will not become a saint.

Obedience gives us inward joy and peace. Obedience is the only condition for close union with God.

We want to become holy and therefore we have to be thoroughly obedient. God never takes from us what we are not willing to give. We must give it to him with our own free will.

For our obedience to be cheerful and prompt, we have to be convinced that it is Jesus we obey. And how do we reach that conviction? By the practice of the heroic virtue of obedience—

love for love. If you want to know whether you love God, ask yourselves the question: "Do I obey?" If I obey, everything is alright. Why? Because everything depends on my will. Whether I become a saint or a sinner depends on me. So you see how very important obedience is. Our sanctity, after the grace of God, depends upon our will. Don't waste time waiting for big things to do for God. You will not have the readiness to say yes to the great things if you do not train yourselves to say yes to the thousand-and-one occasions of obedience that come your way throughout the day.

Something happened to one of the sisters who was sent to study. The day she was to receive her degree she died. When she was dying she asked, "Why did Jesus call me for such a short time?" And her superior answered, "Jesus wants you, not your works." She was perfectly happy after that.

Knowledge of God, love of God, service of God—that is the end of our lives—and obedience gives us the key to it all.

℞

A certain priest loved the Chinese and wanted to do something for them. He became so involved in the work that it seemed that even his eyes became slanted, like the Chinese. If I live constantly in the company of Jesus, I will look like him and do as he did. Nothing pleases God more than when we obey. Let us love God not for what he gives but for what he deigns to take from us. Our little acts of obedience give us the occasion of proving our love for him.

ℚ

It is much easier to conquer a country than to conquer ourselves. Every act of disobedience weakens my spiritual life. It is like a wound letting out every drop of one's blood. Nothing can cause this havoc in our spiritual life as quickly as disobedience.

In the Gospel we find many proofs of Christ's obedience. If we were to go to Nazareth in spirit we would first hear Our Lady's answer to the angel, "Be it done to me according to thy word." Then we would hear this about Jesus: "He went down and was obedient to them"—to a carpenter and a simple village girl. Then we would hear Jesus say: "I have come to do the will of my Father, of him who sent me." At last, we would see Jesus at his passion, obeying his executioners blindly.

We must build our obedience on the example of Jesus in the Gospel. What is this obedience?

By this vow of obedience I give to God something he cannot take from me without my consent: my will, of which I have full control.

To strengthen ourselves to remain obedient, we must refrain from criticism. Anything that weakens my obedience, however small, I must keep away from. If we don't obey, we are like a building without cement. For us, obedience is like cement. Obedience is unreasonable for a proud soul, but there is no unreasonableness in obedience for a humble soul.

Obedience is something that makes me Christlike. What we give up through poverty is something that many people in the world can do. The same is true of chastity. But to love and esteem the privilege of living under obedience is for the few who choose it. Why love and esteem it? Because it is not only a sure means of fulfilling the will of God but is also a very special grace and honor.

What does perfect obedience bring? It is an unfailing source of peace. Inward joy comes only from perfect obedience.

Close union with God is a natural result of perfect obedience.

If we want to do something great for the church, we must first become obedient. Jesus is our model. He was poor, obedient, charitable. "In you, Jesus, I want to be pure; I want to obey; I want to be poor." I cannot say I will find the way. No, I have to give up even my own self so that only Jesus does it in me.

ℛ

Poverty and obedience are very closely united. These complete each other. One cannot be without the other. That is why Scripture says, "He, being rich, became poor." Also, "Behold, I come to do thy will, Oh God." "My food is to do the will of him who sent me." I don't think Jesus would have been able to live his life if he had not accepted this. He had to become poor and to obey his Father fully. He became both materially and spiritually poor. If we are proud and uncharitable, rather than empty, then we cannot really obey.

Obedience is more difficult than poverty. Our will is the only thing we can claim. In poverty nothing is ours. In obedience I have my will, the only thing God will not take by force. The more you love God the more you will obey.

ℛ

Many congregations have discarded this vow of obedience. They don't have superiors anymore. Each member makes her own decisions. They have discarded obedience completely. Do you know what has happened because of that? In the United States alone fifty thousand nuns have left the religious life. The destruction of religious life comes mainly from the lack of obedience. Sheer negligence destroys religious life completely.

ॐ

Obedience is the most perfect act of love for God. I obey not because I am afraid, but because I love Jesus. Then only will I be able to progress very far in sanctity. If I neglect obedience, poverty will go. When poverty goes, chastity will go. Tradition says the angels were told to adore the Christ Child. When Satan said, "I will not serve" that was the first act of disobedience. Even the angels had the chance to choose.

ॐ

"He, being rich, became poor." It is difficult for a proud person to obey. We do not like to bend, to be humble. To be holy we need obedience. The Gospels are full of the humility of Mary. As spotless as she was, as holy as she was, she obeyed. "Humility of the heart of Jesus, fill my heart." Let us, during the day, pray this prayer often. If there has been resentment in our hearts or if we have not accepted humiliation, we will not learn humility. We cannot learn humility from books. Jesus ac-

cepted humiliation. Nothingness cannot dis-
obey. In our lives as Missionaries of Charity,
obedience is the greatest gift we can give to
God. Jesus came to do the will of his Father, and
he did it from the very beginning to the very
end.

If we really want to know whether something
is a temptation, let us examine our obedience. It
is the best light in time of temptation, and we
will know exactly where we are and what we
are doing. It is the best light in that terrible
darkness. Even for Jesus, the devil wanted to
find out who he was. He was not sure. The devil
will stoop to anything to find out where our
weak point is. He will do anything to get us to
accept that one wrong thought, to say that one
unkind word, to do that one impure act, that
one act of disobedience, that one instance of
giving something away without permission,
that one neglect of prayer—just that one thing.
If there is an award to be given for patience it
should be given to the devil. He has a lot of
patience.

This strength we need and must learn from
Jesus. That is why we need the Eucharist. See
how the devil acted with Jesus. He went step by
step; one temptation, then another. He failed,

but he began again. That is why Jesus knew how much we need him, and that is why we should pray. Watch the beginnings. Temptations—like temptations against purity when they come—are only there to help us reach a greater love for purity. Obedience is the protector of all the vows and virtues. That is why we make our vows according to obedience. The devil does not care what thing he tempts us to do as long as we are not preoccupied with Jesus.

ℚ

One of the doorways to holiness is obedience. To be able to obey, we must be free. That is why we take a vow of poverty, having nothing. Jesus came down and was subject. We must go down in the depths of our hearts and see how to bring holiness into our society.

ℚ

Many times Jesus said: "I have come to do the will of my Father. I and the Father are one." In the Old Testament when did God punish? When his people did not obey; when they did not keep their word to him.

ℚ

How long was Jesus subject? Thirty long years. He had come to give the good news, and yet he spent thirty years doing the work of a carpenter. He was called the "son of a carpenter."

~

Examine your poverty. Is it something joyful? Examine your obedience. Is your obedience total surrender? They are twins. Poverty is the sister and obedience is the brother. If you know poverty and obedience, you will love them. If you love them, you will keep them.

~

Difficult, yes. It's meant to be difficult. Jesus says: "If you want to be my disciple, pick up your cross and follow me." He doesn't force us. He says, "if you want." We are not the only ones that have to obey. Even taxi drivers have to obey. Red light, green light, that's also obedience.

I've never received so many graces as through obedience. You will receive many more graces if you surrender totally.

Love for obedience is love for the will of God.

~

Rome, July 16, 1965

And *all* the superiors of our society, I call you to be what our Holy Father said in public—the servant of the servants of God. You are to serve and not to be served; the word "co-workers" fits each one of you more than any other sister. Remember, you are first for the sisters. Help them to grow to be Christlike. Know each sister better. Then you will love her and only then will you serve her with a devoted love, as Christ loved each one of us.

ॐ

Obedience well lived frees us from selfishness and pride and so it helps us to find God and, in him, the whole world. Obedience is a special grace, and it produces unfailing peace, inward joy, and close union with God.

Obedience transforms small, commonplace things and occupations into acts of living faith, and faith in action is love, and love in action is service of the loving God. Obedience lived with joy creates a living awareness of the presence of God, and so fidelity to acts of obedience become like drops of oil that keep the light of Jesus aflame in our life.

WHOLEHEARTED, FREE SERVICE TO THE POOREST OF THE POOR

Our consecrated service to the poorest of the poor is Christ's call to us through his church,

  — to love him wholeheartedly and freely in the

poorest of the poor with whom he identifies himself and makes his presence in them known, loved, and served by all.
— to make reparation for sins of hatred, coldness, lack of concern and love for him in the world today, in one another, and in the person of the poorest of the poor.

Ꝛ

By this vow we bind ourselves to give wholehearted and free service to the poorest of the poor according to obedience.
— Wholehearted means: with hearts burning with zeal and love for souls, with singleminded devotion, wholly rooted in our deep union with God in prayer and fraternal love, that we give them not only our hands to serve, but also our hearts to love with kindness and humility, entirely at the disposal of the poor.

Ꝛ

We give immediate and effective service to the poorest of the poor, as long as they have no one to help them, by:
— feeding the hungry: not only with food but also with the Word of God,
— giving drink to the thirsty: not only for water, but for knowledge, peace, truth, justice, and love,
— clothing the naked: not only with clothes, but also with human dignity,

— giving shelter to the homeless: not only a shelter
made of bricks, but a heart that understands, that
covers, that loves,

— nursing the sick and the dying: not only the
body, but also the mind and spirit.

℣

The poorest of the poor, irrespective of caste, creed, or
nationality are: The hungry, the thirsty, the naked, the
homeless, the ignorant, the captives, the crippled, the
leprosy sufferers, the alcoholics, the sick and dying
destitutes, the unloved, the abandoned, the outcasts, all
those who are a burden to human society, who have lost
all hope and faith in life, and every Missionary of
Charity by accepting to live the life of evangelical
poverty and by the very fact of being sinners—and all
hard-hearted, persistent sinners, those under the power
of the evil one, those who are leading others to sin, error
or confusion, the atheists, the erring, those in confusion and doubt, the tempted, the spiritually blind, the
weak, lax, and ignorant, those not yet touched by the
light of Christ, those hungry for the word and peace of
God, the difficult, the repulsive, the rejected, the
sorrowful, and the souls in purgatory.

℣

Our vocation is to follow the lowliness of
Christ. We remain right on the ground by living
Christ's concern for the poorest and the low-
liest and by being of immediate but effective

service to them until they find some others who can help in a better and more lasting way.

✺

As you love God you must love the poor in their sufferings. The love of the poor overflows from your love for God. You must find the poor and serve them. When you have found them, you must take them to your heart. We owe our people the greatest gratitude, because they allow us to touch Christ. We must love the poor like him. A Hindu told me, "I know what you do in *Nirmal Hriday*, you take them from the streets and bring them to heaven."

✺

The difference between our work and social work is that we give wholehearted, free service for the love of God. In the beginning, when the work started, I got a fever and had a dream about St. Peter. He said to me, "No, there is no place for you here. No slums in heaven." "Alright," I answered him, "then I shall go on working. I'll bring the people from the slums to heaven."

✺

Our vocation is not the work—the fidelity to humble works is our means to put our love into action.

"That they may all be one even as you, Father, are in me and I in you: that they also may be one in us, so that the world may believe that you have sent me" (Jn 17:21).

God will take care of you, if you remain one.

❧

As a religious community, modelled on the first Christian community, our first great responsibility is to be community, revealing first to one another something of God's own love, concern, and tenderness—what it means to know and to be known, to love and to be loved, and thus to be a sign witnessing to the deepest vocation of the church, which is to gather people from every tribe and tongue, and people and nation, redeemed by the blood of Christ, to form God's family of love. "See how they love each other."

❧

As members of an international community, we will use English as our community language.

❧

Just as Jesus sent his disciples out two by two, we will also go out two by two with permission and with a sister as a companion. We will pray the rosary on the streets and help each other to fervor and zeal, and we will also protect each other.

The superior of each house, however, will remember that she is first for the sisters and next for the work. Therefore:

— all her dealings with the sisters will be motherly, never discouraging them especially in failure,

— she will encourage and joyfully welcome each member to make a personal and valuable contribution to the well-being of the society and the church. This will lead to wiser decisions that will prove beneficial to all.

— she will always be the first to devote herself to the housework,

— she will have nothing special or different in food, clothes, or lodging;

— she will trust her sisters completely and be generous always, especially when the sisters observe poverty well,

— she will respect with utmost discretion all that the sisters confide in her, and do not wish to be revealed, especially personal matters. She will never force secrets out of them,

— above all, by her own example of humility, obedience, and oneness with her higher superiors, she will teach her sisters the art of doing "always the things that please the Father."

We shall always keep in mind that our community is not composed of those who are already saints, but of those who are trying to become saints. Therefore we shall be extremely patient with each other's faults and failures.

Our love for one another will be:
— selfless, generous, tender, personal, and respectful,
— beyond likes and dislikes, friendship and enmity, worthiness or unworthiness,
— faithful, deep, and freeing,
— not compromising because we care; compassionate and forgiving because we understand,
— always inspiring, encouraging, trusting, wholehearted, and sacrificial unto the death of the cross.

༄

My vows bind me to my sister because she is much poorer than the poor outside. If I am not kind and do not smile to the poor outside, someone else will. But for my sister there is no one else.

༄

Society: the word *societas* is taken from the Spanish military term *campagnia* meaning "company, a cohort of soldiers." Hence it implies the thorough organization of an army. From this we see that in our society there should be no individualism, since all things in an army are in common. Like soldiers we are not to have a fixed residence. Also like soldiers we are to possess that undaunted courage and fearlessness that will meet all perils and dangers with equanimity of soul. A true soldier of this company is ever ready to make any sacrifice, to undertake any toil and labor. The Missionary of Charity is not content with the common lot of a soldier. Her desire is to push on until she comes close to the King—crucified and dying of thirst. There the hand of the true soldier will lift her burning soul to satiate that thirst of her God and King.

ς

Motherhouse, October 4, 1969

In times of weakness, your superior comes and appears as Christ in his distressing disguise—she needs your love, your humility, your trust. Trust her with loving trust, in spite of herself, for Jesus in her has not changed. He is the same, as there is only one Jesus.

Our society is still young. Our superiors are still without much experience. Have compassion on them, be kind to them. See the hand of the good God that is trying to write a wonderful message of love to you personally using that bad pencil, maybe even a broken pencil. Even so, it is the hand and mind of God, and you must try to understand and refrain from examining the pencil. Today he uses the pencil which is rough and yet the loving message is there—always beautiful, always true, always thoughtful—only for you. Christ will use only that pencil in the place you are—for you. Therefore, kiss the hand, but do not try to break the pencil.

OUR LIFE TOGETHER

As a sign of entrance into a new state of life by religious consecration and as a sign of our desire for self-effacement:
- *we receive a new religious name at the time of profession,*
- *we call each other "sister."*

Our Religious dress consists of:
- *a simple and modest white cotton habit,*
- *a white cotton sari with blue border covering the head,*
- *a cincture made of rope,*
- *sandals,*
- *a crucifix and a rosary.*

These will be the sign of:
— *our consecrated love for God and the church,*
— *our dedication to the world's poor, and*
— *a reminder of the edification expected from all those who wear it.*

Candidates desirous to join the Society must be:
— *at least eighteen years of age,*
— *free from impediments,*
— *guided by the right intention,*
— *healthy in body and mind, and hence able to bear the hardships of this special vocation,*
— *able to acquire knowledge (especially the language of the people they serve),*
— *of a cheerful disposition,*
— *able to exercise sound judgment.*

The sisters shall wear a plain Indian dress, that is a white habit, a white sari with blue par, a girdle made of rope, a crucifix, and sandals.

The white habit and a sari with blue border is the sign of Mary's modesty; it should remind me of my separation from the world and its vanities, of my baptismal robe and how pure I must keep my heart.

The girdle made of rope is the sign of Mary's angelic purity. It should remind me that I should aim at the same purity helped by the strong guardian, Holy Poverty.

Sandals are a sign of freedom; of our own free choice we follow Christ in search of souls.

The crucifix is a sign of love—the sign we should know, love, and imitate. When I dress myself I should, with devotion, remember what each article of my religious habit means to me. Therefore, I should say each prayer with great love.

Yes, our dress is a sign that we belong—that is why we must take great care. This habit is a protection for us, both bodily and spiritual protection. Be grateful for the habit.

৶

The work we have to do requires a healthy body. Therefore, each sister is in her conscience bound to take care of her health. The amount of food, which is very wisely prescribed for us, must be taken faithfully. This we do, not for the satisfaction of the senses, but to show our Lord our desire to work for him and with him, that we may be able to live lives of penance and reparation.

৶

It would be a defect to speak about food or to complain about what is served. To be occupied with such thoughts at any time is not edifying. If dishes taste well, thank God! If not, thank him still, and thank him even more because he has given you an opportunity to imitate our Savior in his poverty. Christ certainly did not feast sumptuously during his life. His parents were poor, and the poor do not feast on the good things of the table. In fact, he often endured real want, as the multiplication of the loaves and fishes and the plucking of the ears of corn on walks through the fields teach us. These incidents should be salutary reminders to us when our meals are meager.

❦

To join the congregation we need few things. We need health of mind and body. We need the ability to learn. We need plenty of common sense and a cheerful disposition. I think common sense and cheerfulness are very necessary for a work like this.

❦

June 1, 1972

As traveling expenses are becoming very high, we have decided in future to take with us, besides our clothes—only our pillow, pillowcase, two sheets, one blanket, a glass, a cup, and one dinner plate. The rest will be provided for you in each house. (Things should be numbered one, two, three, etc.—everything numbered number one will go to one sister; number two will go to the next sister; and so on. This means that each house should have things according to the number of members in the house.)

Once a month you must all help clean the godown where food and relief goods are kept. All the sisters in the house must know what you have to give to the poor, but one sister must be responsible for giving it rather than every-one giving at random. Also, it would be good for everyone, including the superior—to clean drains and toilets at least once a week and to give a helping hand in the kitchen. Wherever there is a plot of land, make sure you work in the garden and plant as many fruit trees as possible so that you can give food to the poor. This will help you return to the spirit of hard labor and sacrifice which has always char-acterized the society.

We have been called to give until it hurts. Our constitution says that "as a sign of our con-secration we receive a new name." We vow to give ourselves to God completely, and our new name expresses that vow. Our name is called and we answer: "Lord, you have called me." The moment we stop hearing our name being called we will be separated from him. We can recognize his voice calling our name only in the silence of our hearts. Changing our names shows that we belong not to ourselves but to Jesus.

Never lose the chance to become like Jesus. We profess before the world, "I am the spouse of Jesus crucified." Like the woman at the altar who professes before the world her marriage to one man, we, too, change our name to show that we belong to Jesus completely.

FOUR

Our Life of Prayer and Contemplation

Lord, teach us to pray. **Lk 11:1**

❧

JESUS HAS DRAWN US TO BE SOULS OF PRAYER

Jesus is our prayer, and he is also the answer to all our prayer. He has chosen to be himself in us the living song of love, praise, adoration, thanksgiving, intercession, and reparation to the Father in the name of the whole creation, especially the poorest of the poor and those who do not pray, who do not know how to pray, who do not dare and do not want to pray.

❧

Every Missionary of Charity will pray with absolute trust in God's loving care for us. Our prayer will be the prayer of little children, one of tender devotion, deep reverence, humility, serenity, and simplicity.

ℛ

By daily feeding on the Scriptures, particularly the New Testament, we shall grow in a deeper and more personal knowledge and love of Jesus Christ and his teachings, so as to be able to feed his children with his divine Word.

We shall be painstaking and diligent in studying and memorizing selected passages, daily reading and meditating on the Scriptures—to be able to know and love God personally.

One with the church in her celebration of the mystery of our redemption, we also promote devotion in accordance with the liturgy and liturgical seasons.

— Devotion to the Sacred Heart of Jesus is closely linked with the Eucharist and has a special place in our society. We renew each year the consecration of our communities on the feast of the Sacred Heart. Every First Friday of the month will be preceded by a novena.

— In gratitude to Jesus for his great love during his passion which is being continued today in his suffering poor, we shall make the Stations of the Cross every Friday as a community. Other days it will be left to the choice of each sister.

ℛ

Singing is an important part of our life of prayer. We shall keep our singing simple and use a minimum of musical instruments when necessary.

ℚ

We are called to be contemplatives in the heart of the world by:
— *seeking the face of God in everything, everyone, everywhere, all the time, and his hand in every happening, and especially,*
— *seeing and adoring the presence of Jesus in the lowly appearance of bread, and in the distressing disguise of the poor, by praying the work, that is, by doing it with Jesus, for Jesus, and to Jesus.*

ℚ

Our life of contemplation shall retain the following characteristics:
— *missionary: by going out physically or in spirit in search of souls all over the world.*
— *contemplative: by gathering the whole world at the very center of our hearts where the Lord abides, and allowing the pure water of divine grace to flow plentifully and unceasingly from the source itself, on the whole of his creation.*
— *universal: by praying and contemplating with all and for all, especially with and for the spiritually poorest of the poor.*

Jesus Christ has told us that we ought "always to pray and not to faint." St. Paul says, "pray without ceasing." God calls all men and women to this disposition of heart—to pray always. Let the love of God once take entire and absolute possession of a heart; let it become to that heart like a second nature; let that heart suffer nothing contrary to enter; let it apply itself continually to increase this love of God by seeking to please him in all things and refusing him nothing; let it accept as from his hand everything that happens to it; let it have a firm determination never to commit any fault deliberately and knowingly or, if it should fail, to be humbled and to rise up again at once, and such a heart will pray continually.

ॐ

People today speak much about the poor, but they do not know or talk to the poor. So, too, we can talk much about prayer and yet not know how to pray.

We have to feed ourselves. We can die from spiritual starvation. We must be filled continually, like a machine. When one little thing in the machine is not working, then the whole machine is not working properly.

We need oil for the lamp.

Our lives must be connected with the living Christ in us. If we do not live in the presence of God, we cannot go on.

℞

Does your mind and your heart go to Jesus as soon as you get up in the morning? This is prayer, that you turn your mind and heart to God. In your times of difficulties, in sorrows, in sufferings, in temptations, and in all things, where did your mind and heart turn first of all? How did you pray? Did you take the trouble to turn to Jesus and pray, or did you seek consolations?

Has your faith grown? If you do not pray, your faith will leave you. All those priests and religious who left, first stopped praying and then lacked faith to go on.

Ask the Holy Spirit to pray in you. Learn to pray, love to pray, and pray often. Feel the need to pray and to want to pray.

If you have learned how to pray, then I am not afraid for you. If you know how to pray, then you will love prayer—and if you love to pray, then you will pray. Knowledge will lead to love and love to service.

℞

Where can I learn to pray? Jesus taught us: "Pray like this: Our Father ... Thy will be done

. . . Forgive us as we forgive." It is so simple yet so beautiful. If we pray the "Our Father" and live it, we will be holy. Everything is there: God, myself, my neighbor. If I forgive, then I can be holy and can pray . . . all this comes from a humble heart, and if we have this we will know how to love God, to love self, and to love your neighbor.

This is not complicated, and yet we complicate our lives so much, by so many additions. Just one thing counts: to be humble, to pray. The more you pray, the better you will pray. How do you pray? You should go to God like a little child. A child has no difficulty expressing his little mind in simple words which say so much. Jesus said to Nicodemus: "Become as a little child." If we pray the gospel, we will allow Christ to grow in us.

One thing is necessary for us—confession. Confession is nothing but humility in action. We used to call it penance, but really it is a sacrament of love, a sacrament of forgiveness. That is why confession should not be a place in which to talk for long hours about our difficulties. It is a place where I allow Jesus to take away from me everything that divides, that destroys. When there is a gap between me and Christ, when my love is divided, anything can come to fill the gap. We should be very simple and childlike in confession. "Here I am as a child going to her Father." If a child is not yet spoiled and has not learned to tell lies, he will tell everything. This is what I mean by being childlike. Confession is a beautiful act of great love. Only in confession can we go as sinners with sin and come out as sinners without sin.

℘

If you don't pray, your presence will have no power, your words will have no power. If you pray, you will be able to overcome all the tricks of the devil. Don't believe all the thoughts that he puts into your mind.

℘

Motherhouse, October 1978

"Blessed are those who suffer persecution": We do not suffer much persecution, except the persecution caused by the devil against chastity, poverty, obedience, and wholehearted free service. To resist this persecution we need continual refilling of prayer and sacrifice—of the Bread of Life, of the Living Water, of my sisters in community, and of the poor. We need Our Lady, our mother, to be with us always, to protect us and keep us only for Jesus.

Prayer enlarges the heart until it is capable of containing God's gift of himself. Ask and seek and your heart will grow big enough to receive him and keep him as your own.

MARY'S EXAMPLE

"Behold your Mother" (Jn 19:27).
Immaculate Heart of Mary, cause of our joy, bless your own Missionaries of Charity.

෴

The Magnificat is Our Lady's prayer of thanks. She can help us to love Jesus best; she is the one who can show us the shortest way to Jesus. Mary was the one whose intercession led Jesus to work the first miracle. "They have no wine," she said to Jesus. "Do whatever he tells you," she said to the servants. We take the part of the servants. Let us go to her with great love and trust. We are serving Jesus in the distressing disguise of the poor.

෴

Through all the work we do for Jesus, with Jesus, to Jesus, we will ask him to deepen our love for his mother, to make it more personal and intimate, so as to:
— love her as he loved her,

— *be a cause of joy to her as he was,*
— *keep close to her as he kept close,*
— *share with her everything, even the cross, as he did when she stood near him on Calvary.*

SILENCE

"Behold, I will allure her and will lead her into the wilderness and I will speak to her heart" (Hos 2:16, 18).
Souls of prayer are souls of great silence.

ᚬ

Each one of us will take it as our serious and sacred duty to collaborate with one another in our common effort to promote and maintain an atmosphere of deep silence and recollection in our own lives, conducive to the constant awareness of the Divine Presence everywhere and in everyone, especially in our own hearts and in the hearts of our sisters with whom we live in the poorest of the poor.

ᚬ

To make possible true interior silence, we shall practice:
— *Silence of the eyes, by seeking always the beauty and goodness of God everywhere, closing it to the faults of others and to all that is sinful and disturbing to the soul.*
— *Silence of the ears, by listening always to the*

voice of God and to the cry of the poor and the needy, closing it to all the other voices that come from the evil one or from fallen human nature: e.g., gossip, tale-bearing, and uncharitable words.

— Silence of the tongue, by praising God and speaking the life-giving Word of God that is the Truth that enlightens and inspires, brings peace, hope, and joy and by refraining from self-defense and every word that causes darkness, turmoil, pain, and death.

— Silence of the mind, by opening it to the truth and knowledge of God in prayer and contemplation, like Mary who pondered the marvels of the Lord in her heart, and by closing it to all untruths, distractions, destructive thoughts, rash judgment, false suspicions of others, revengeful thoughts, and desires.

— Silence of the heart, by loving God with our whole heart, soul, mind, and strength and one another as God loves, desiring God alone and avoiding all selfishness, hatred, envy, jealousy, and greed.

Our silence is a joyful and God-centered silence; it demands of us constant self-denial and plunges us into the deep silence of God where aloneness with God becomes a reality.

To foster and maintain a prayerful atmosphere of exterior silence we shall:

— *respect certain times and places of more strict silence,*
— *move about and work prayerfully, quietly and gently,*
— *avoid at all costs all unnecessary speaking and notice,*
— *speak, when we have to, softly, gently, saying just what is necessary,*
— *look forward to profound silence as a holy and precious time, a withdrawal into the living silence of God.*

℣

If we will only learn silence, we will learn two things: to pray and to be humble. You cannot love unless you have humility, and you cannot be humble if you do not love. From the silence of the heart God speaks. There is no silence if there are things that have got inside.

℣

Regarding purity, Jesus said, "Blessed are the clean of heart, for they shall see God." If our hearts are filled with uncharitableness and jealousy, we cannot see God. I can spend hours in church, but I will not see God if my heart is not pure. That is why we need silence. In the silence of the heart God speaks and in the purity of the heart God speaks.

Silence of our eyes.

Silence of our ears.

Silence of our mouths.

Silence of our minds.

Silence of our hearts.

For in the silence of the heart God will speak. Give Jesus these five silences as a token of your gratitude. You will never learn to pray until you keep silence:

The fruit of silence is faith.

The fruit of faith is prayer.

The fruit of prayer is love.

The fruit of love is service.

And the fruit of service is silence.

The fourth vow is the fruit of silence. If you don't pray you cannot be a Missionary of Charity—you will be a social worker.

❧

Silence of the *heart,* not only of the mouth—that too is necessary. Then you can hear God everywhere: in the closing of the door, in the person who needs you, in the birds that sing, in the flowers, the animals—that silence which is wonder and praise. Why? Because God is everywhere, and you can see and hear him. That crow is praising God. That stupid crow—I can hear it well. We can see and hear God in that crow, but we cannot see and hear him if our heart is not clean.

ॽ

He who spoke with authority now spends his earthly life in silence. Let us adore Jesus in the eucharistic silence. We need to find God, and he cannot be found in noise and restlessness. See how nature, the trees, the flowers, and the grass grow in perfect silence. See the stars, the moon, and the sun, how they move in silence. The apostle said, "We will give ourselves continually at prayer and to the ministry of the Word." For the more we receive in silent prayer, the more we can give in our active life. We need silence to be able to touch souls. The essential thing is not what we say, but what God says to us.

ॽ

If we are careful of silence it will be easy to pray and to pray fervently. There is so much talk, so much repetition, so much carrying of tales in words and in writing. Our prayer life suffers so much because our hearts are not silent, for as you know "only in the silence of the heart, God speaks." Only after we have listened can we speak from the fullness of our hearts.

꩜

"God is the friend of silence. His language is silence." Be still and know that I am God. He requires us to be silent to discover him. In the silence of the heart, he speaks to us.

Jesus spent forty days before beginning his public life in silence. He often retired alone, spent the night on the mountain in silence and prayer. He who spoke with authority spent his early life in silence.

We need silence to be alone with God, to speak to him, to listen to him, to ponder his words deep in our hearts. We need to be alone with God in silence to be renewed and to be transformed. Silence gives us a new outlook on life. In it we are filled with the grace of God himself, which makes us do all things with joy.

PRAYING THE WORK

"I pray not only for these but for those who through their words will believe in me" (Jn 17:20).

Pray and work daily that all may become followers of Christ.

❧

We shall pray our work, but we may not substitute our prayer by work.

Besides praying for the whole world, especially for the spiritually poorest of the poor, each sister will be assigned a specific prayer mission on the level of the universal and local church, nations, our own society, the poor we serve all over the world, and the families and individuals we visit locally (for the contemplative sisters).

❧

Faith in action is service. We try to be holy because we believe. In most modern rooms you see an electrical light that can be turned on by a switch. But, if there is no connection with the main power house, then there can be no light. Faith and prayer is the connection with God, and when that is there, there is service.

❧

The only thing Jesus has asked us to be is meek and humble of heart, and to do this, he has taught us to pray. He has put "meek" first. From that one word comes gentleness, thoughtfulness, simplicity, generosity, truthfulness. For whom? For one another. Jesus put "humility" after meekness. We cannot love one another unless we hear the voice of God in our hearts.

᠖

If only we could understand what it is "to pray the work." If we could only deepen our faith. Prayer is not just time spent and words uttered. If only our faith were as big as a mustard seed, we would be able to tell this thing to move and it would move. . . . if our hearts are not pure we cannot see Jesus in others.

᠖

If we neglect prayer and if the branch is not connected with the vine, it will die. That connecting of the branch to the vine is prayer. If that connection is there then love is there, then joy is there, and we will be the sunshine of God's love, the hope of eternal happiness, the flame of burning love. Why? Because we are one with Jesus. If you sincerely want to learn to pray: keep silence.

᠖

What have we to learn? To be meek and humble; if we are meek and humble we will learn to pray. If we learn to pray, we will belong to Jesus. If we belong to Jesus we will learn to believe, and if we believe we will learn to love, and if we love we will learn to serve.

ॐ

Be sincere in your prayers. Do you pray your prayers? Do you know how to pray? Do you love to pray? Sincerity is nothing but humility and you acquire humility only by accepting humiliations. All that has been said about humility is not enough to teach you humility. All that you have read about humility is not enough to teach you humility. You learn humility only by accepting humiliations. And you will meet humiliation all through your lives. The greatest humiliation is to know that you are nothing. This you come to know when you face God in prayer. When you come face to face with God, you cannot but know that you are nothing, that you have nothing. In the silence of the heart God speaks. If you face God in prayer and silence, God will speak to you. Then you will know that you are nothing. It is only when you realize your nothingness, your emptiness, that God can fill you with himself.

When you become full of God, you will do all your work well, all of it wholeheartedly. We have our fourth vow of wholehearted service: it means to be full of God. And when you are full of God, you will do everything well. This you can do only if you pray, if you know how to pray, if you love prayer, and if you pray well.

❧

Your vows are nothing but worship of God. If you are sincere in your prayers, then your vows have meaning; otherwise, they will mean nothing. The taking of your vows is also a prayer because it is worship of God. Your vows are between you and God alone. There is no one in between. It is all between Jesus and you.

Spend your time in prayer. If you pray you will have faith, and if you have faith you will naturally want to serve. The one who prays cannot but have faith, and when you have faith you want to put it into action. Faith in action is service. Faith in action becomes a delight because it gives you the opportunity of putting your love for Christ into action—it is meeting Christ, serving Christ.

❧

You need especially to pray, for in our society, the work is only the fruit of prayer ... our love in action. If you are really in love with Christ, no matter how small the work, it will be done better; it will be wholehearted. If your work is slapdash, then your love for God is slapdash. Your work must prove your love.

Prayer is the very life of oneness, of being one

with Christ.... Therefore, prayer is as necessary as the air, as the blood in our body, as anything to keep us alive—to keep us alive to the grace of God.

ℒ

It is impossible to engage in the apostolate without being a soul of prayer, without a conscious awareness of and submission to the divine will. We must be aware of our oneness with Christ, as he was aware of his oneness with his Father. Our activity is truly apostolic only in so far as we permit him to work in and through us—with his power, his desire, his love. We must become holy, not because we want to *feel* holy, but because Christ must be able to live his life fully in us.

Prayer must come from the heart and must be able to touch the heart of God. See how Jesus taught his disciples to pray: Call God your Father; praise and glorify his name; do his will as the saints do it in heaven; ask for daily bread, spiritual and temporal; ask for forgiveness of your own sins and for the grace to forgive others; ask for the grace to resist temptations and for the final grace to be delivered from the evil which is in you and around you.

These words of Jesus, "Love one another, even as I have loved you," should be not only a light to us, but they should also be a flame consuming the selfishness which prevents our growth in holiness. Jesus loved us to the end, "to the very limit of love, to the cross." This love must come from within—from our union with Christ. It must be an outpouring of our love for God. Loving must be as normal to us as living and breathing, day after day until our death. To understand this and practice it we need much prayer, the kind that unites us with God and overflows continually upon others. Our works of charity are nothing but the overflow of our love of God from within. Therefore, the one who is most united to him loves her neighbor most.

FIVE

Our Life of Service and Evangelization

Whatsoever you do to the least of my brethren, you do it to me. **Mt 25:40**

ℛ

FAITH IN ACTION IS LOVE
LOVE IN ACTION IS SERVICE

No work should be introduced or accepted which is not in conformity with the aim of the society. As the society and all its members must be free to go in search of souls, to carry God's love among the poorest of the poor, it follows that we will have no regular schools, no boarding schools, no hospitals, no nursing homes except those homes needed for the homeless destitutes and the unwanted.

In the slums the sisters should find a place where they will gather little street children, whoever they may be. Their very first concern is to make them clean, feed them and only then teach them, and prepare them for admission into regular schools. The love of God must be proposed to them in a simple, interesting, and attractive way.

ૡ

The sisters shall visit the destitute and the sick, going from house to house or wherever these may be found, and they must render to all the humblest services. They shall also visit the jails.

We shall:
— *call sinners to repentance,*
— *instruct the ignorant,*
— *counsel the doubtful,*
— *sustain the tempted,*
— *befriend the friendless and comfort the sick and sorrowful,*
— *bear wrongs patiently: trusting in God for deliverance in his own good time,*
— *forgive injuries,*
— *bring prayer into the lives of the spiritually poorest of the poor.*

ૡ

We need to be pure of heart to see Jesus in the person of the poorest of the poor. Therefore, the more repugnant the work, or the more disfigured or deformed the image of God in the person, the greater will be our faith and loving devotion in seeking the face of Jesus, and lovingly ministering to him in the distressing disguise.

℞

St. Theresa of Lisieux said, "Our Lord has need of our love. He has no need of our works. The same God who declares that he has no need to tell us if he be hungry, did not disdain to beg a little water from the Samaritan woman. He was thirsty, but when he said, 'Give me to drink,' he, the creator of the universe, asked for the love of his creature. He thirsted for Love."

℞

The true interior life makes the active life burn forth and consume everything. It makes us find Jesus in the dark holes of the slums, in the most pitiful miseries of the poor—the God-Man naked on the cross, mournful, despised by all, the man of suffering crushed like a worm by the scourging and the crucifixion. This interior life motivates the Missionary of Charity to serve Jesus in the poor.

℞

We must work in great faith, steadily, efficiently, and above all with great love and cheerfulness, for without this our work will be only the work of slaves, serving a hard master.

ॐ

It is him we serve in the poor; it is for his sake that we become beggars. How great will be our joy when at the last judgment we will hear our Lord address his Missionaries of Charity with these words, "Come ye blessed of my Father, inherit the kingdom prepared for you from the foundation of the world. For I was hungry and ye gave me to eat, thirsty and ye gave me to drink. I was a stranger and ye brought me within, naked and ye clothed me. I was sick and ye visited me, in prison and ye came unto me . . . in as much as ye did it to one of the least of these my brethren, ye did it to me."

ॐ

However beautiful the work is, be detached from it—even ready to give it up. You may be doing great good in one place, but obedience calls you elsewhere. Be ready to leave. The work is not yours. You are working for Jesus. Obedience and humility are one and the same thing. If you want to know whether you are humble, ask yourself, "Do I obey because I see Christ in every command? Poverty one can get used to, but every act of obedience is an act of the will, and it gets harder as we grow older

because we get our own ideas. Every humiliation is a sacrifice.

❧

You may be exhausted with work—you may
even kill yourself—but unless your work is
interwoven with love, it is useless.

❧

Don't give in to discouragement. No more
must you do so when you try to settle a
marriage crisis or convert a sinner and don't
succeed. If you are discouraged, it is a sign of
pride because it shows you trust in your own
powers. Never bother about people's opinions.
Be humble and you will never be disturbed. It is
very difficult in practice because we all want to
see the result of our work. Leave it to Jesus.

❧

Never do the work carelessly because you
wish to hide your gifts. Remember, the work is
his. You are his co-worker. Therefore, he depends on you for that special work. Do the
work with him, and the work will be done for
him. The talents God has given you are not
yours—they have been given to you for your
use, for the glory of God. There can be no half-
measures in the work. You may feel very bad,
but feelings are not the measure of our love for

Christ. It is our will and our work that matters.
Be great and use everything in you for the good
Master.

THE WORK IS NOT OURS

Remember the work is not ours and we must
not spoil it. That would be a great injustice to
God because the work is his. It is better that the
whole society be wiped out than that God's
work be spoiled.

℞

We love him in the distressing disguise.
Otherwise there is no meaning in being a
Missionary of Charity. Our society goes deeper.
It is the hungry Christ I feed. Christ is really in
the poor.

℞

We have to love our vocation. I must really
say: Christ lives in me. I must be able to say that.
We have to keep on desiring. The desire will
only be fulfilled when we are face to face with
God. Here on earth we must have that desire to
live with Christ in the poor. Jesus said "I was
hungry, you gave me to eat. I was thirsty and
you gave me to drink. I was ignorant and you
taught me. You took me to church." This is not

simply something to excite our imagination. Jesus really said it. So he is the poor we meet everywhere.

꒦

We are the servants of the poor. We give wholehearted, free service to the poor. In the world the people are paid for their work. We are paid by God. We are bound by a vow to love and serve the poor, and to live as the poor with the poor.

꒦

St. Ignatius said, "I must do my work as if everything depends on me—and the result I leave to God." The people in the world take so much trouble—we also must do the same. They work for hours to make themselves attractive. We must make ourselves attractive to God.

꒦

We must do better than the people in the world, because we do it for Jesus. If we find it difficult, we should ask Jesus to give us a drop from his precious blood.

There is a story of a little robin. He saw Jesus on the cross, saw the crown of thorns. The bird flew around and around until he found a way to remove a thorn—and in removing the thorn it struck him. Each one of us should be that bird.

What have I done; what comfort have I given? Does my work really mean something?

The little robin tried to remove just one thorn. When I look at the cross, I think of that robin. Don't pass by the cross—it is a place of grace. The cross—hands seared with pain. Did I put compassion in my hands for one who was sick? How did I touch my patient?

&

For money people do so much work in the world. I want you to do your work well for the greater glory of God. What does it matter whether the whole world knows of the Missionaries of Charity? That does not change anything. But we must want the poor to get the best things that others get for money.

&

I don't need numbers. I need Missionaries of Charity full of love, full of zeal. God has entrusted us with a very special thing: to be his love and compassion to the poorest of the poor. You can't do that if you are not holy.

&

No Missionary of Charity is called to do big things. Our work sounds big because there are so many little things, but when you look at it, there is nothing to show—nothing. I was so happy to see a sister cleaning the toilets, because they were shining. She must have cleaned them with great love and done it in the presence of God.

~

If something belongs to me, I've got full power to use it as I want. I belong to Jesus; he can do to me whatever he wants. The work is not our vocation. I can do this work without being a religious. Can you tell me why we become Missionaries of Charity? The work is not our vocation. Our vocation is to belong to him. Our profession is that we belong to him. Therefore, I am ready to do anything: wash, scrub, clean. I am like a mother who gives birth to a child. The child belongs to her. All her washing, staying up at night, and so on is proving that the child belongs to her. She will not do this for any other child, but she will do anything for her own child. If I belong to Jesus, I will do anything for Jesus.

~

The child is the fruit of married love. How beautiful! God has said: "Let man and woman be created for that purpose."

The Church is the spouse of Jesus, and for us

Missionaries of Charity the fruit of that oneness with Jesus is the poor. Just as the fruit of mother and father is the child, so the fruit of my relationship with Jesus and me is the poor. Today ask yourself: "What is the fruit of my vow of chastity?"

❧

Mary said: "Let it be done according to thy word." Then she went in haste. See her total surrender. This is why Our Lady is a Missionary of Charity in the true sense of the word. Each morning I, too, must go in haste: I am going to have an audience with God. Each morning I receive Jesus: his blood, his body in my body. Then what happens? Our Lady spent nine months with Jesus; Jesus was in her . . . and what did she do? Scrub, clean, wash, but she really loved her total surrender. I have to do the same. In the street I must go in haste, burning with love and zeal to give Jesus to the poor.

❧

Let the praise of people not destroy the peace in our hearts and make us restless. It has been given to us; let us give it back to him with great love. They cannot give praise to all. It has been given to One—but it has been given to the lepers, the children, dying patients—to all in him. All that work is only a drop in the ocean, but if we neglect to put in that drop, the ocean will be less.

✣

As you know, we have our brothers who are also Missionaries of Charity. One of our brothers loves the lepers. We are taking care of forty-nine thousand lepers in India. This brother really loves the lepers. He came one day after he had had some difficulties with his superior. He said to me, "I love the lepers; I want to be with them. I want to work for them. My vocation is to be with the lepers." I said to him, "Brother, you are making a mistake. Your vocation is not to work for the lepers. Your vocation is to belong to Jesus. The work for the lepers is only your love for Christ in action; and, therefore, it makes no difference to anyone as long as you are doing it to him, as long as you are doing it with him. That's all that matters. That is the completion of your vocation, of your belonging to Christ."

✣

A sister was telling me that just two or three weeks ago she and some other sisters picked up a man from the streets in Bombay and brought him home. We had a big place donated to us which we have turned into a home for the dying. This man was brought there and the sisters took care of him. They loved him and treated him with dignity. Right away they discovered that the whole of his back had no skin, no flesh. It was all eaten up. After they washed him they put him on his bed, and this sister told me that she had never seen so much joy as she saw on the face of that man. Then I asked her, "What did you feel when you were removing those worms from his body; what did you feel?" And she looked at me and said, "I've never felt the presence of Christ; I've never really believed the word of Jesus saying, 'I was sick and you did it to me.' But his presence was there and I could see it on that man's face." This is the gift of God.

I insist on saying that we are not social workers. We are really contemplatives in the heart of the world.

A LITTLE PENCIL IN GOD'S HAND

A Missionary of Charity is just a little instrument in the hands of God. We must try to keep it always like that—being just a small instrument in his hands. Very often I feel like a little pencil in God's hand. He does the writing; he does the thinking; he does the movement—I have only to be a pencil and nothing else.

— You are being sent; you have not chosen for yourself where you want to go; and you are *sent* just as Jesus was *sent* to us.

— You are sent not to teach but to learn: learn to be meek and humble of heart. That is just what Jesus has asked us to do: "Learn of me for I am meek and humble of heart."

— You are sent to serve and not to be served: Go to serve with a humble heart. Never escape the hard work. Be always the first one to do it.

— Go to be a cause of joy to your communities.

— Go with zeal and love for the poor.

— Go in haste, like Our Lady, to serve.

— Choose the hardest thing. Go with a humble heart, with a generous heart. Don't go with ideas that don't fit into our way of life: with big, big ideas about theology and what you would like to teach, but rather go to learn and to serve.

— Share what you have received, with a humble heart.

— Go to the poor with great tenderness. Serve the poor with tender, compassionate love.

— Say yes to peace with your tongue. Close your mouth rather than speaking a word which will hurt anyone.

—Go to give yourselves without any reservation. Give yourselves wholeheartedly, unreservedly.

ℛ

Have I really learned to pray the work? Maybe I have never learned to pray the work because the whole time my mind is on "work." Here are words that will help you: "With Jesus, for Jesus, to Jesus." If you want to know how much you love Jesus, there is no need to ask anybody to tell you. In the sincerity of your heart you will know, if you practice silence.

ℛ

You have done a lot of work these days; it was nicely done, but did you give what was inside of you? What did that giving mean to you? Did you give with love and respect? If you did not pray that giving it was just a giving of self.

Did the people see you give with love and respect? Did you give the medicine with faith to the sick Christ? This is the difference between you and the social worker.

ℛ

I will pick the roses. The sharper the thorns, the sweeter shall be my song. For the aim of joining is not to become social workers. Our work is not a profession, but a vocation chosen to satisfy the thirst of Jesus by total surrender, without counting the cost.

ຉ

We must know that we have not come here to be numbers. I want Missionaries of Charity and not just workers. With money I can get workers. I want each of us to be able to say, "I work for the poor because I love God."

"I was hungry and I waited for you but you did not come. I was homeless on the street. I waited for you but you did not come." Jesus will judge us on this. Somebody told me that we are the only ones in the whole church of God with this fourth vow of charity. We must be conscious of this, sisters. We have a special responsibility to the church to fulfill this special call.

Sisters, don't look for big things, just do small things with great love.

ຉ

Motherhouse, July 18, 1968

Feeding the hungry Christ.
Clothing the naked Christ.
Visiting the sick Christ.
Giving shelter to the homeless Christ.
Teaching the ignorant Christ.

We all long for heaven where God is, but we have it in our power to be in heaven with him right now—to be happy with him at this very moment. But being happy with him now means loving like he loves, helping like he helps, giving as he gives, serving as he serves, rescuing as he rescues, being with Him twenty-four hours a day—touching him in his distressing disguise.

We need to realize that we have the privilege of touching Jesus twenty-four hours. When I'm feeding that child, I'm feeding Jesus. Think a little. Elizabeth did not know—but the child John the Baptist jumped in her womb. The same thing should happen when our slum people meet us. "That sister—she has compassion. She is giving Holy Communion, giving medicine as if she were giving Holy Communion."

ᘒ

Lent, 1975

Each time Jesus wanted to prove his love for us, he was rejected by mankind. Before his birth his parents asked for a simple dwelling place and they were given none because they were poor. The innkeeper probably looked at Joseph the carpenter and decided that he would not be able to pay. So he refused. But Mother Earth opened a cave and took in the Son of God.

Again, before the redemption and the resurrection, Jesus was rejected by his people. They did not want him—they wanted Caesar; they did not want him—they wanted Barabbas. At the end, it was as if his own Father did not want him because he was covered with our sins. In his holiness he cried, "My God, my God why hast thou forsaken me?"

Yesterday is always today to God. Therefore, today in the world Jesus stands covered with our sins, in the distressing disguise of my sister, my brother. Do I want him? If we are not careful, soon the riches of the worldly spirit will become an obstacle. We will not be able to see God, for Jesus has said: "Blessed are the clean of heart, for they shall see God."

People rejected Jesus because his poverty was hurting their riches. My sisters, do our poor reject us because our riches hurt their poverty? Are they at ease with us because we are so like them in poverty? Can we look straight in the face of the poor and say with a sincere heart: "I know poverty; she is my companion. I love poverty; she is my mother. I serve poverty; she is my mistress."

Motherhouse, July 3, 1978

Begin the leprosy and medical work with a prayer and put in a little more gentleness, a little more compassion for the sick. It will help you to remember that you are touching the body of Christ. He is hungry for that touch. Will you not give it?

៷

To become a saint one must suffer much, and to love much we must suffer more. Suffering begets love, but it is also fruitful because it begets life for souls. How full of love we must be in order to be true to our name.

៷

Yesterday has gone, tomorrow has not yet come and we have only today to make him known, loved, and served.

THE POOR WE SERVE

Our children may be only slum children, but for that very reason just anything will not do. Each sister must find a way to attract, to capture the hearts of the children. Don't think that you need not prepare the lessons because you know more than they. They must have the best, and their good must be uppermost in your mind. Don't get stale in your methods, like stagnant water. Keep on improving yourself. Try new ways and means. You may have the knowledge, but you must also know how to impart it.

Our children come to school with empty stomachs—don't waste their time. They must learn something—to be able to read and write a little and tell a little about the life of our Lord. Make them happy. They have had much to suffer already, and we cannot treat them as we would children going to a regular school.

❧

Be kind, very kind, to the suffering poor. We little realize what they go through. The most difficult part is the feeling of not being wanted. This is the first hardship a leper experiences, even today. Show your love for them by being very kind—act kindly, speak kindly. I prefer our sisters to make mistakes through kindness than to work miracles through harshness and unkindness.

❧

In Addis Ababa, where the government is expelling missionaries in a few hours notice, the Governor said to me, "Even if I have to send away everyone else, yet I will not let your sisters go, because I know and see that the sisters love and care for our poor people."

❧

All over the world people are saying that Mother Teresa is spoiling the poor by giving them things free. At a seminary in Bangalore, once a nun said to me, "Mother Teresa, you are spoiling the poor people by giving them things free. They are losing their human dignity." When everyone was quiet, I said calmly, "No one spoils as much as God himself. See the wonderful gifts he has given us freely. All of you here have no glasses, yet you all can see. If God were to take money for your sight, what would happen? Continually we are breathing and living on oxygen that we do not pay for. What would happen if God were to say, 'If you work four hours, you will get sunshine for two hours'? How many of us would then survive?" Then I also told them: "There are many congregations who spoil the rich; it is good to have one congregation in the name of the poor, to spoil the poor." There was profound silence; nobody said a word after that.

꙰

Do we treat the poor as our dustbins to give whatever we cannot use or eat? I cannot eat this food so I will give it to the poor. I cannot use this thing or that piece of cloth so I will give it to the poor. Am I then sharing the poverty of the poor? Do I *identify* myself with the poor I serve? Am I one with them? Do I share with them as

Jesus shared with me?

This is the wonderful part of our vocation, that as Missionaries of Charity we have created an awareness of the poor in the whole world. Twenty years ago no one would believe that there were hungry, naked men and women around. Today the whole world knows our poor because of our work. Because they know they want to share.

The other day, a group of Hindu school children came from very far. They had won prizes in a contest at school and had asked the headmistress to give them money instead of the prizes. Then they said, "Now, take us to Mother Teresa. We want to give this money to her poor people." How wonderful it was that they did not use that money for themselves! Because we have created this awareness the whole world wants to share with the poor. Whenever I accept money or an award, I always take it in the name of the poor, whom they recognize in me. What am I? I am nothing. It is the poor whom they recognize in me and that they want to give to, because they see what we do. Today people in the world want *to see*. Why is our congregation spread all over the world today? It is because people see what we do: feeding the hungry Christ, clothing the naked Christ, taking care of the sick, the dying, the leprosy patients. Because they see, they believe. How sad it will be if we are not sincere in what we do.

٭

Our poor people suffer much, and unless we go with joy we cannot help them. We will make them more miserable.

٭

Among the poor we have the rich poor— children with more gifts, patients who are able to clean themselves, and so on. We must be careful not to pick and choose. There are children who are mentally retarded, who cannot respond to you, and so you may neglect those. This is where we have the duty of wholehearted, free service. The "rich" poor child can still have a place but it is the child so retarded and hungry, for whom I must especially work.

٭

At home, we must love our sisters. They too are—the poorest of the poor. Afterwards it will be easy outside.

٭

Our poor people are becoming poorer day by day. Be a comfort to the poor and take every trouble to help them. Open your eyes to the needs of the poor. Put into reality the words "to give wholehearted, free service to the poor." Give to Christ in his distressing disguise. It is Jesus in the poor that you feed, clothe, and take in. Do it all with a great, undivided love.

※

Our sisters are working in New York with the shut-ins. They see the terrible pain of our people, the pain of loneliness, of fear, of being unwanted and unloved. I think it is much greater pain, much greater than even cancer or tuberculosis. The sisters have often met people like that, people who are completely broken-hearted, desperate with feelings of hurt.

※

Sometime ago a man came to our house and said: "Mother, there is a Hindu family that has eight children. They have not eaten for a long time. Do something for them." So I took some rice and went. When I arrived at their house, I could see the hunger in the children's eyes. Their eyes were shining with hunger. I gave the rice to the mother. She took it and divided it into two, and then she went out. When she came back, I asked her, "Where did you go?" She said, "They are hungry also." Her neighbors were also hungry. What struck me most was not that she gave the rice but that she knew they were hungry. Because she knew, she shared. I did not bring more rice that night. I waited until the next morning so that they could experience the joy of sharing and loving.

Love, to be true, has to hurt, and this woman who was hungry—she knew that her neighbor was also hungry. That family happened to be a Muslim family. It was so touching, so real. This is where we are most unjust to our poor—we don't know them. We don't know how great they are, how lovable, how hungry for that understanding love. Today God loves the world through you and through me. Are we that love and that compassion? God proves that Christ loves us—that he has come to be his Father's compassion. Today God is loving the world through you and through me and through all those who are his love and compassion in the world.

ର

God has been pouring many graces into the congregation, and I think we owe deep gratitude to the poor. Their life of suffering, their life of prayer, their life of tremendous forbearance obtains many graces for us. Also, there are all those thousands of people who have died in our hands. I am sure they pray much for us when they go to heaven. The whole thing is nothing extraordinary, nothing special. It has been just a simple surrender, a simple yes to Christ, allowing him to do what he wants. That is why the work is his work. I'm just a little pencil in his hand. Tomorrow, if he finds somebody more helpless, more stupid, more hopeless, I think he will do still greater things with her and through her.

ॐ

Jesus is reliving his passion in our poor people. The poor are really going through the passion of Christ. We should treat them with dignity. These poor people are Jesus suffering today. We must find ways and means of helping them; don't add to their sufferings. Poor people are living Jesus' Calvary today.

OUR LIFE OF EVANGELIZATION

The special aim of the society is to labor at the conversion and sanctification of the poor in the slums; that is, by nursing the sick and the dying, by gathering and teaching little street children, by visiting and caring for beggars and their children, by giving shelter to the abandoned.

To labor at the conversion and sanctification of the poor in the slums involves hard, ceaseless toiling, without results, without counting the cost. . . . To convert and sanctify is the work of God, but God has chosen the Missionaries of Charity in his great mercy to help him in his own work. It is a special grace granted to the Missionaries of Charity, without any merit of theirs, to carry the light of Christ into the dark holes of the slums.

"I have other food to eat that you know not of. Lift up your eyes and see the fields, white and ready for the harvest" (Jn 4:32-35). This is my food, the conversion and sanctification of souls.

ᢣ

When we do "our work," visiting the families, teaching the children, nursing the sick, helping the dying, gathering the little children for church, we should do it with one aim in view: "the salvation of the poor." We want to bring them to Jesus and bring Jesus to them.

The knowledge we impart must be that of Jesus crucified. St. Augustine says: "Before allowing his tongue to speak, the apostle ought to raise his thirsting soul to God, and then give forth what he has drunk in and pour forth what he has been filled with."

Zeal for souls is the effect and the proof of true love of God. If we really love God, we cannot but be consumed with the desire of saving souls, the greatest and the dearest interest of Jesus. Therefore, zeal is the test of love and the test of zeal is devotedness to his cause—spending our life and energy in the work for souls.

❧

We have to carry our Lord to places where he has not walked before. Therefore the sisters must be consumed with one desire: Jesus. Speak of no one but him crucified. We must not be afraid to do the things he did—to go fearlessly through death and danger with him and for him.

A "missionary" carries the interest of Christ continually in her heart and mind. In her heart there must be the fire of divine love and of zeal for God's glory and for the salvation of souls. This love makes her spend herself without ceasing. This becomes her real object in life and her joy.

The missionary must die daily, if she wants to bring souls to God. She must be ready to pay the price he paid for souls, to walk in the way he walked.

Our holy faith is nothing but a gospel of love,

revealing to us God's love for men and women and claiming in return their love for God. "God is love." A missionary must be a missionary of love. We must spread God's love on earth if we want to make souls repent wholeheartedly for sin, strengthen them against temptation, increase their generosity and their desire to suffer for Christ. Let us "act Christ's love among men and women," remembering the words of the *Imitation of Christ,* "Love feels no burden, values no labours, would willingly do more than it can, complains not of impossibility because it conceives that it may and can do all things; when weary is not tired; when straightened is not constrained, when frightened is not disturbed; but like a lively flame and a torch all on fire, it mounts upwards and securely passes through all oppositions."

Love has a hem to her garment that reaches to the very dust. It sweeps the stains from the streets and lanes, and because it can, it must. The Missionaries of Charity, in order to be true to their name, must be full of charity in their own souls and spread that same charity in the souls of others—Christians and pagans.

॥

If you give to the people a broken Christ, a lame Christ, a crooked Christ—deformed by you, that is all they will have. If you want them to love him, they must know him first. Therefore, give the whole Christ—to the sisters, first, then to the people in the slums. Do I give the Christ who is full of zeal, love, joy, and sunshine? Do I come up to the mark? Or am I a dark light, a false light, a bulb without connection, having no current and therefore shedding no radiance? Put your heart into being a bright light. "Help me to shed thy fragrance everywhere I go."

Let the poor, seeing you, be drawn to Christ. Poverty makes people very bitter, and they speak and act without realizing what they do. But do they remember Christ when they see you—even if they get angry—because you remind them of Christ?

Draw them to God but never, never to yourself. If you are not drawing them to God, then you are seeking yourself, and people love you for yourself and not because you remind them of Christ.

❧

The surest way to preach Christianity to the pagan is by our cheerfulness, our happiness. What would our life be if the sisters were unhappy? It would be slavery and nothing else. We would do the work but we would attract nobody.

The sister must have one thing clear: there is a soul to save, a soul to bring to God. The sister has to be extremely kind and gentle; in touch of hand, in tone of voice, in her smile—for the work is very delicate. Nirmal Hriday (a hospital run by the Missionaries of Charity) is a treasure house; so is every hospital. An unkind word or look is enough to spoil the work. Such perfection of charity is not in us but we must acquire it—kindness in action. You will not learn kindness by looking after sick people unless you practice it on healthy people, because the sick are often trying and hard to please.

❧

What is the good news? The good news is that God still loves the world through each one of you. You are God's good news, you are God's love in action. Through you, God is still loving the world.

❧

Recently, one great Brazilian man, a man of high position, wrote to me that he had lost faith in God and man. He gave up his position and everything and only wanted to commit suicide. One day, as he was passing by a shop, his eyes suddenly fell on a TV in the window. There was the scene of Nirmal Hriday, the sisters looking after the sick and dying. He wrote to me that after seeing that scene, he knelt and prayed for the first time in many years. Now he has decided to turn back to God and have faith in humanity because he saw that *God still loves the world*—he saw this on TV.

೮

A rich couple came to see me the other day. They had been to Nirmal Hriday. The man told me that when he saw the sisters caring for the dying something clicked in his heart. He said that he would never be the same man again. What clicked? I do not know, but he met God's love in action and something clicked in his heart, so he cannot be the same man again.

೮

Once a man came to Kalighat, right into the ward. I was there. After a little while he came back and said to me, "I came here with so much hate in my heart, hate for God and hate for man. I came here empty, faithless, embittered, and I saw a sister giving her wholehearted attention to a patient, and I realized that God still loves. Now I go out a different man. I believe there is a God and that he loves us still." Often we do our work slapdash because we do not have enough faith. If we truly believe we are doing it to Jesus we will do our work well.

❦

Once, someone asked me, "Why do you go abroad? Don't you have enough poor in India?" So I answered, "I think Jesus told us to go and preach to all the nations." That is why we go all over the world to preach his love and compassion.

❦

When our sisters were in Ceylon, a minister of state once told me something very surprising. He said, "You know, Mother, I love Christ but I hate Christians." So I asked him how that could be. He answered, "Because Christians do not give us Christ; they do not live their Christian lives to the full." Gandhi said something very similar, "If Christians were to live their Christian lives to the full, there would not be one Hindu left in India." Isn't it very true? This love of Christ should urge us to spend ourselves without ceasing.

❦

Mulvi, a Muslim, was standing with Father Gabric and watching a sister bandaging the wound of a leper with great love. She didn't say anything, but she did something. He turned to Father and said, "All these years I believed that Jesus was a prophet, but today I know he is God because he has given so much love into the hands of this sister." Even today, that sister does not know that her action brought Jesus into the life of that man.

ॐ

"The light, Oh Jesus, will be all from you— none of it will be mine. It will be you shining on others through me. Shine through me and be so in me that every soul I come in contact with may feel your presence in my soul. Let them look up and see Jesus."

ॐ

The joy of Jesus will be my strength—it will be in my heart, in every person I meet. They will see it in my work, my walk, my prayer—in everything.

ॐ

At the opening of Baroda (a Hindu festival) a group of Hindu came to me and said: "You have come to convert us?" I looked at them and smiled and said, "Naturally, that's the treasure I have; I would like you to be Christian, but I will not force it on you. Even God cannot force himself on anyone who does not want him."

Faith is a gift. Let us not humiliate the Hindus by saying, "For a plate of rice you give up your religion." Christianity is a living reality. It is a search, and we must desire it and find God.

༄

Very often we pick up sick and dying destitutes from the streets of Calcutta. In twenty-five years we have picked up more than thirty-six thousand people from the streets and more than eighteen thousand have died a most beautiful death. When we pick them up from the street like that, we give them a plate of rice. In no time we revive them. A few nights ago we picked up four people. One was in a most terrible condition, covered with wounds, her body full of maggots. I told the sisters that I would take care of her while they attended to the other three. I really did all that my love could do for her. I put her in bed and then she took hold of my hand. She had such a beautiful smile on her face and she said only: "Thank you." Then she died. There was a greatness of love. She was hungry for love, and she received that love before she died. She spoke only two words, but her understanding love was expressed in those two words. I have never seen a smile like that.

୧

Yesterday, a sister was telling me about some sisters who go to the prison. They take the Blessed Sacrament, and the prison chaplain has started daily adoration for half an hour. To see those prisoners, young boys and men, adoring. They are preparing some of those boys for First Communion. They're hungry for God—they are very hungry for God. That man who we picked up from the streets said, "I have lived like an animal in the street but I'm going to die like an angel." I can tell you that of the eighteen thousand that have died in Calcutta alone, I've not seen one of them die in distress. Nobody has died in despair. It is so beautiful. We feel this is the fruit of our vocation, of our oneness with Christ. We need that continual feeding; that is why we begin the day at half past four in the morning and then we have Mass, Holy Communion, and meditation.

୧

May, 1964

To children and to the poor, to all those who suffer and are lonely—give them always a happy smile; give them not only your care but also your heart.

Kindness has converted more people than zeal, science, or eloquence. We take a vow to give wholehearted service to the poor. Does this not mean love of the poor? The poor are not at our service. If we want the poor to see Christ in us, we must first see Christ in the poor.

ॽ

Let us preach the peace of Christ like he did; he went about doing good. He did not stop his works of charity because the Pharisees and others hated him or tried to spoil his Father's work. He just went about doing good. Cardinal Newman wrote: "Help me to spread thy fragrance everywhere I go; let me preach thee without preaching, not by words but by my example—by the catching force, the sympathetic influence of what I do, the evident fullness of the love my heart bears to thee." Our works of love are nothing but works of peace. Let us do them with greater love and efficiency. It is always the same Christ who says:

I was hungry—not only for food, but for peace that comes from a pure heart.

I was thirsty—not for water, but for peace

that satiates the passionate thirst of passion for war.

I was naked—not for clothes, but for the beautiful dignity of men and women for their bodies.

I was homeless—not for a shelter made of bricks, but for a heart that understands, that covers, that loves.

Motherhouse, May 1975

When you look at the inner workings of electrical things, often you see small and big wires, new and old, cheap and expensive lined up. Until the current passes through them there will be no light. That wire is you and me. The current is God. We have the power to let the current pass through us, use us, produce the light of the world—Jesus. Or we can refuse to be used and allow darkness to spread.

Our Lady was the most wonderful wire. She allowed God to fill her to the brim. By her surrender "Be it done to me according to thy word" she became "full of grace." The moment she was filled by this current, by the grace of God, she went in haste to Elizabeth's house to connect the wire, John, to the current, Jesus. As his mother said, "This child, John, leapt up with joy at your voice." Let us ask Our Lady to come into our lives also and make the current, Jesus, use us to go round the world—especially in our own communities so that we can continue connecting the wires of the hearts of men and women with the current, Jesus.

CHARITY MUST COST US

The more repugnant the work, the greater the effect of love and cheerful service. If I had not first picked up that woman who was eaten up by rats—her face, and legs, and so on—I could not have been a Missionary of Charity. But I returned, picked her up, and took her to Camphel Hospital. If I had not, the society would have died. Feelings of repugnance are human. If we give our wholehearted, free service in spite of such feelings, we will become holy. St. Francis of Assisi was repulsed by lepers but he overcame it. He died; but Christ lives.

There was a queen, St. Elizabeth of Hungary, who was a holy person, but her husband was rather cruel. Yet she treated him as she would treat Christ. She had a mother-in-law who was jealous of the love her son bore his wife. One day Queen Elizabeth offered hospitality to a leper and even gave him her husband's bed to lie on. The mother-in-law, seeing this, seized the opportunity to set her son against his wife. The husband dashed angrily into the room but to his surprise he saw the figure of Christ on the bed. Elizabeth could have acted thus only because she was convinced she was doing it to Christ himself. We must therefore be proud of our vocation which gives us the opportunity to serve Christ in his poorest. It is in the slums that we must seek to go and serve Christ.

At the altar how gently and tenderly the priest touches the consecrated host, with what love he looks at it. The priest believes that the host is the disguise of Jesus. In the slums Jesus chooses as his disguise the miseries and poverty of our people. You cannot have the vow of charity if you have not got the faith to see Jesus in the people you meet. Otherwise our work is no more than social work. . . . What if you feel a disgust and run away? Feelings don't count. Run away but come back without delay.

Charity, to be fruitful, must cost us. Actually, we hear so much about charity. Yet we never give it its full importance: God put the commandment of loving our neighbor on the same footing as the first commandment. God's love is infinite. God has prepared us for service, so he expects this from us. He has given each of us something that in one way or another will enable him to shine through us.

We want to be something for Almighty God, and since we cannot reach God and do it directly to him, we serve him in the poor people of India. We are here purely for the love of God. Our charity must be true. We must feel in our very bones that we are doing it—we should be living fires of love. Every Missionary of Charity must be like a burning bush. Love to be true must hurt. It must be something I want to give—cost what it may.

೪

Today, in the words of our Holy Father, each one of us must be able "to cleanse what is dirty, to warm what is lukewarm, to strengthen what is weak, to enlighten what is dark." We must not be afraid to proclaim Christ's love and to love as he loved. In the work we have to do, no matter how small and humble it may be, we must make it Christ's love in action. Do not be afraid to proclaim his poverty. Do not be afraid to go with Christ and be subject to those who have authority from above and so declare Christ's obedience unto death. Rejoice that once more Christ is walking through the world, in you and through you, going about doing good.

v

When he showed his heart to St. Margaret Mary, Jesus said again and again, "Love me as I have loved you." "Impossible," she said, "the only way I can do it is if you take my heart and give me yours." Let us ask Jesus sincerely, "Let me share your loneliness, your being unloved, uncared for." Do something today to share in the passion. Maybe Jesus is asking something of you in a special way, maybe something small. If he is not asking you, it might be because you are holding very tightly to something. He will never force it out of you. Maybe he wants you just to smile, to say "May I," to be on time, or to give up an unhealthy friendship.

v

"My child, receive the symbol of our crucified spouse. Follow his footsteps in search of souls. Carry him and his light into the homes of the poor, especially to the souls most in need. Spread the charity of his heart wherever you go and so satisfy his thirst for souls." These words express beautifully the whole of our life. If we just live this, we will be holy; we will be spouses of Jesus crucified.

We must not imagine that we will be crucified with nails. Crucifixion, sisters, is when something hurts me and I hurt back. I say a cruel word and I put a nail into somebody's heart. Nobody, but God, knows how big the nails were, but we know that Jesus was crucified. If you are in pain, see in your pain that pain of Jesus, your loneliness in his loneliness. Spread the charity of his heart wherever you go.

~

Suffering will come, trouble will come—that's part of life—a sign that you are alive. If you have no suffering and no trouble, the devil is taking it easy. You are in his hand.

If I am the spouse of Jesus crucified, he has to kiss me. Naturally, the nails will hurt me. If I come close to the crown of thorns, it will hurt me. If a man leaves his father and mother and clings to his wife, they become one. They cleave to each other. If I am one with Jesus, it must hurt when I share his sorrow.

~

Rome, October 10, 1980

What delicate love God has had for the poor of the world to have created the Missionaries of Charity. You and I have been called by our name, because he loved us. Because you and I are somebody special to him—to be his heart to love him in the poor, his hands to serve him in the poorest of the poor. My children, how much love and care we must take of him—if only we were in love with him. Let us learn to pray the work to be able to be twenty-four hours with Jesus, to do it for Jesus and to Jesus. We need a pure heart, a heart that is filled with nothing but Jesus.

To be a co-worker means to work along with someone, to share together in tiredness, humiliations, and shame, not only in success. Those who share everything are partners, giving love for love, suffering for suffering. Jesus, you have died, you have given everything, your life blood, all. Now it is my turn. I put everything into the field also. The common soldier fights in the way, but the devoted one tries to be near the captain to share his fate. This is the only truth. . . . The only thing that matters—for it is the spirit of Christ.

He wants to live his life in you, to look through your eyes, walk with your feet, love with your heart. In Christ and through Christ, hear Jesus, your co-worker speak to you. "I want you to be my fire of love among the poor, the sick, the dying, and the little children—the poor I want you to bring to me."